Dedicated to the Memory of
Adela Catherine Breton
1849 - 1923

THE ART OF RUINS

Adela Breton & the Temples of Mexico

Edited by
Sue Giles and Jennifer Stewart

Catalogue produced in conjunction with the exhibition
The Art of Ruins: Adela Breton and the Temples of Mexico
City of Bristol Museum and Art Gallery,
16 December 1989 - 10 March 1990

Published by City of Bristol Museum and Art Gallery, 1989
Typeset by Brian Smith Partnership, Bristol
Paper by James McNaughton Group, Avonmouth, Bristol
Printed by TL Visuals Ltd., Bristol
Designed by Steve Russell, City of Bristol Museum and Art Gallery

ISBN 0 900199 38 5

Frontispiece:
Photograph of Adela Breton and Pablo Solorio. Much of the travelling she did in Mexico was on horseback, always riding side-saddle. Ea 11507

Front Cover:
View of the Pyramid of the Niches at El Tajín, a Classic period site in Veracruz State. Ea 8125, Cat.No.38

Contents

Simplified Chronological Table

showing areas, cultures and some sites mentioned in the text. Dates are approximate, and are likely to be changed by current and future archaeological, epigraphical and historical research.

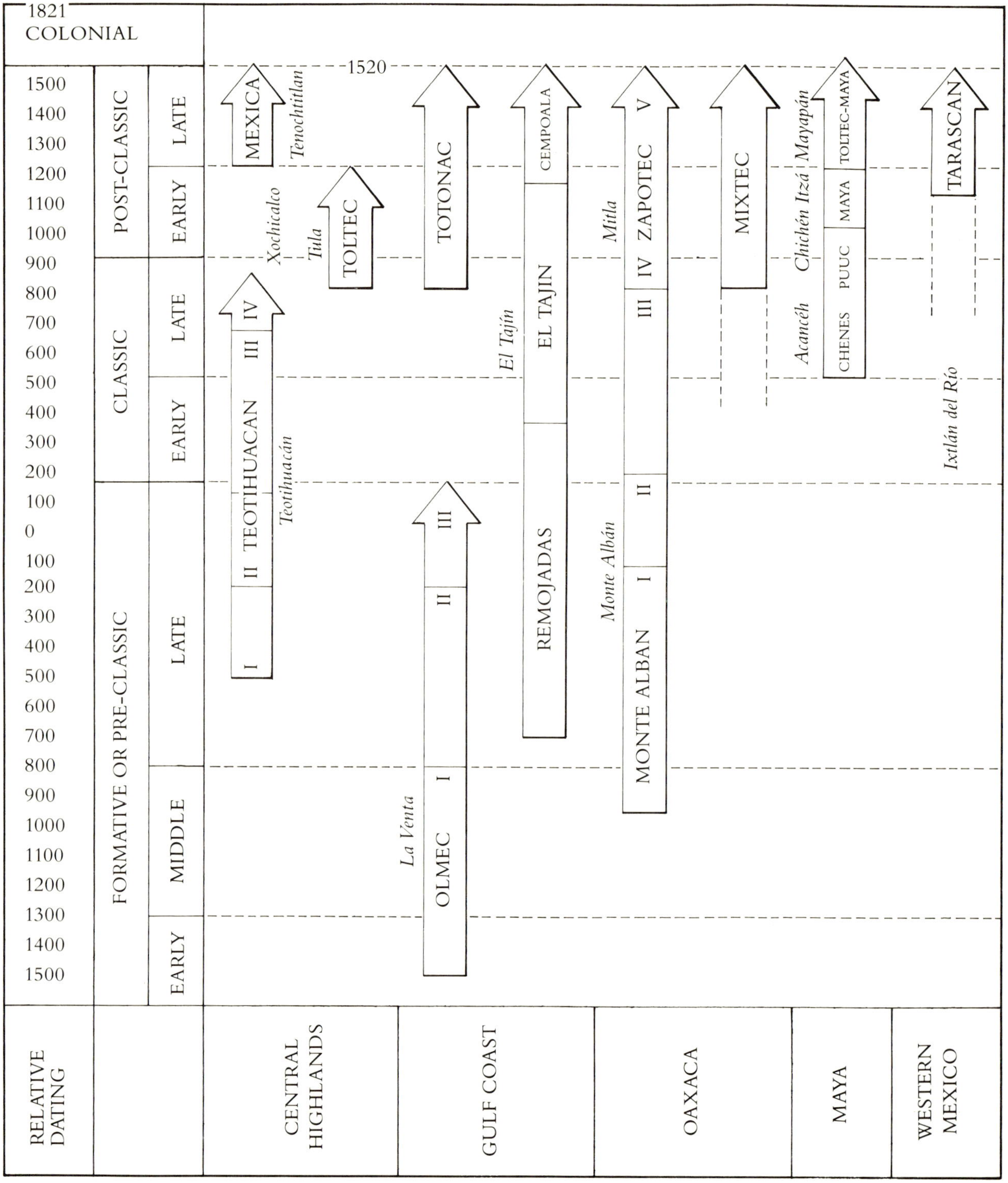

Introduction

The idea of staging an exhibition on the life and work of Adela Breton is not new: a display was mounted at Bristol Museum in 1946. It was not until recently, however, that it was feasible to mount a major exhibition, publish a catalogue and arrange a national tour of the Breton collection. This was due to the help and support of many people whom we would like to acknowledge here.

Our aim in both the exhibition and the catalogue is to show how the dedication, stamina and hard work of a little known Victorian traveller and artist has given us a unique archive of images - sketchbooks, watercolours and photographs - of the splendour and colour of Mexican architecture. Taken together with her small collection of antiquities and extracts from her conversational letters, the archive gives us an intriguing view of how Adela Breton led her life. How many of us, I wonder, could put up with the rigours of 'basic' living, the hazardous travel and the grinding hard work to which she subjected herself, time after time, on her visits to Mexico at the turn of the century ?

We hope to convey the debt owed to Adela Breton for her work; much of the architectural decoration she recorded is now lost, which makes the preservation of the archive so important today.

Many people helped in many ways in preparing the exhibition and its catalogue: we apologise to any who have been overlooked.

First and foremost, our thanks to the contributors to the publication, listed below, who have all been most co-operative throughout the editorial process. Much of the information presented here is new: we are privileged that they have allowed us to publish these details in our catalogue.

Elizabeth Carmichael and Anita Schrader (Museum of Mankind) and Dr Warwick Bray (University of London) helped with aspects of Mexican archaeology. The Congress of Americanists, the Peabody Museum of Archaeology and Ethnology and Harvard University Archives most generously allowed us to publish material from their holdings. Mrs Sue Brothers was instrumental in locating much of this archive material. In the preparation of the text our thanks go to Gail Boyle, Nick Dixon, Kate Osborne, Maria Trowbridge, Linda Langley, Elisa Towlson, and especially to Gideon Spoonbill for the compilation of the index.

To the Bristol Magpies, Ed Carter and David Sproxton, our grateful thanks for funding and practical help towards Sue Giles' field trip to Mexico in the spring of 1989.

We are indebted to Phoebe Beedell and in particular Steve Russell for the care and skill they devoted to designing the exhibition and catalogue, and to the other design staff for their technical assistance.

We are grateful to the Museums and Galleries Commission (Michael Sixsmith), the Area Museum Council for the South West (Richard de Peyer) and the Somerset

County Museum Service (David Dawson) for financial and practical help and enthusiasm in arranging the national and regional tours.

We received financial assistance from a number of sources and companies including Gleeds, Bales and the Bristol Magpies.

For help and assistance among the Museum staff our particular thanks go to Nicholas Thomas, and to Brian Boyd, Fiona MacAllister, Carol Brown, Andy Cotton, Roger Clarke and Philippa Burrell; also to Sarah Watkins, Judith Philpott, Nancy Mortimer-Rudd and Mary Campbell.

As all museum people know, the organising of exhibitions can be exhilarating, if exhausting, so I must dedicate my last but deepest thanks to three stalwart members of my team who, despite gentle nagging, maintained a happy enthusiasm and love of the project: Gail Boyle, Gideon Spoonbill and especially Sue Giles, for all of her hard work in co-editing the texts and skill in arranging the exhibition.

Jennifer Stewart
Curator of Archaeology
December 1989

Contributors

Sue Giles
Assistant Curator of Archaeology, City of Bristol Museum and Art Gallery

Dr James Langley
Research Associate, Institute of Archaeology, University of London

Dr Virginia E. Miller
American Embassy, Madrid

Mary Frech McVicker
Free-lance author, Naperville, Illinois

Dr Hasso von Winning
Consultant in Meso-American Archaeology, Southwest Museum, Los Angeles

Foreword

Adela Breton's reputation has suffered more than most from the pendulum-like swings of archaeological fashion. In her lifetime she knew all the great names in Meso-American studies; Tozzer, Putnam, Bowditch, Zelia Nuttall, Maudslay and Seler regularly figure in her correspondence, and she was a respected member of the small, but international, group of scholars who laid the foundations of Maya archaeology. By the 1960s she was almost forgotten. *The Handbook of Middle American Indians*, the definitive compendium of its day, lists only three of her articles, and the new generation of authors all but ignored her work.

These were the years when Maya archaeology was establishing itself as a 'scientific' discipline and was trying to shake off the preoccupation with fine art and monumental architecture which runs through Adela Breton's diaries and letters. Today art history has become respectable again. Epigraphers are reconstructing historical events from Maya inscriptions, and the representational scenes (from the miniatures painted on pottery to the large scale wall paintings and carved monuments) are providing new insights into the Maya mind, the world of politics, mythology, ritual and belief systems. Adela Breton's accurate copies of architectural decoration show details that have disappeared over the years or have been damaged beyond repair, and her archive in Bristol now attracts visitors from all over the world.

It is the drawings and paintings that established her reputation, but we should not ignore the rest of the Breton collection, which is full of interesting bits and pieces. Several years ago, for example, when I was looking for specimens of pre-Hispanic Mexican silverwork, I could find only one item in Britain. It was a silver disc from the Breton collection and it came from Churumuco - perhaps even from that 'nice little collection of antiquities' brought to her by Pablo Solorio from his home village in Michoacan.

By a happy coincidence the invitation to write this foreword arrived when I was in Yucatán, visiting many of the sites discussed in the catalogue. At Chichén Itzá the noise of the camera shutters and the polyglot clatter of international tourism has replaced the sound of 'the tall grass... making music in the wind', and at Oxkintok a Spanish excavation team was busily at work. But the lesser sites have not changed much since the early years of the century. At Acanch the Acropolis temple was deserted, but over the years the stucco frieze has deteriorated in spite of its tin roof. Inevitably, my camera failed; for teaching purposes I am still using a drawing made from photographs taken by Adela Breton more than eighty years ago.

Warwick Bray
Institute of Archaeology
University of London
December 1989

Major sites in Central America

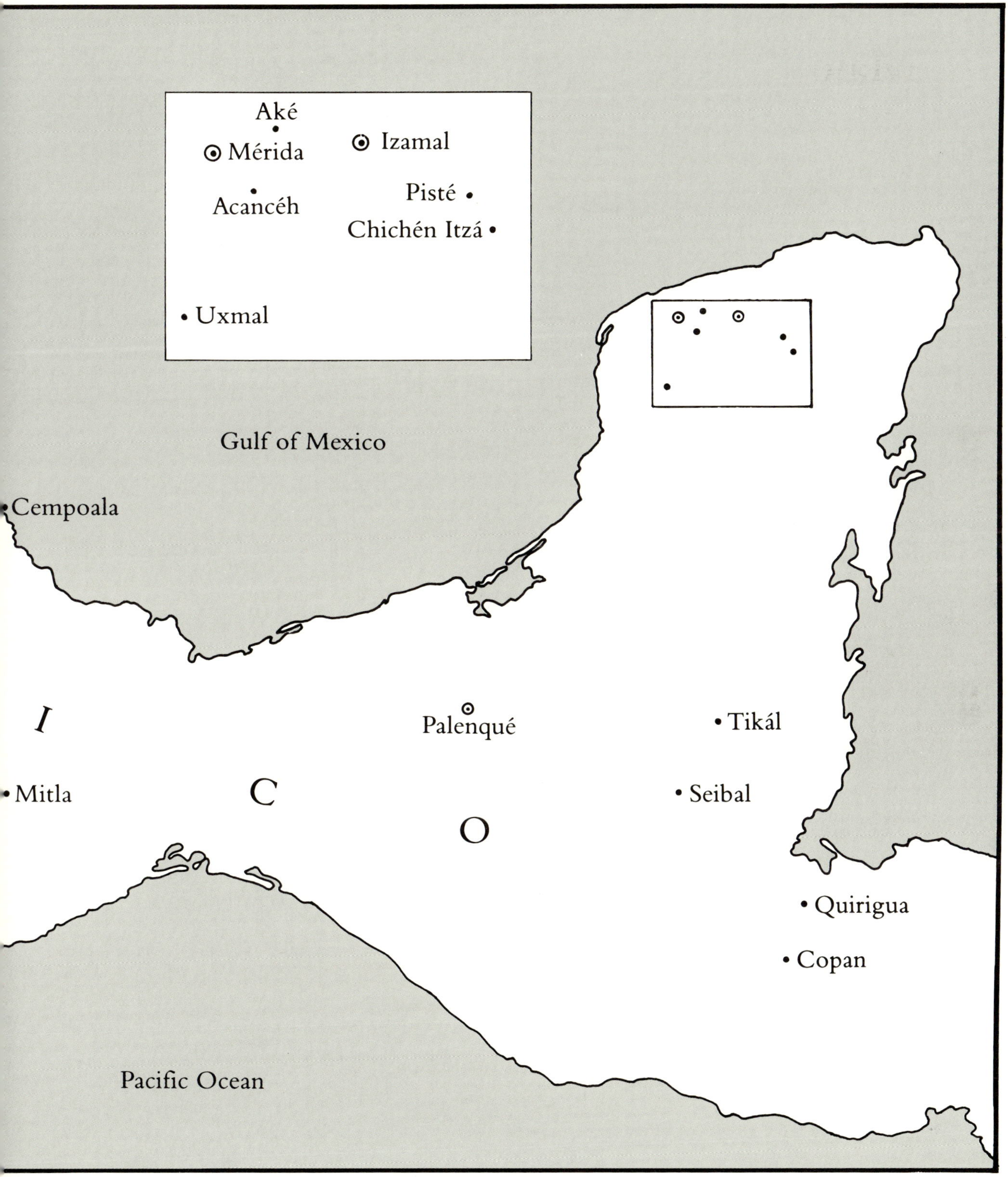

Aké
Mérida
Izamal
Acancéh
Pisté
Chichén Itzá
Uxmal
Gulf of Mexico
Cempoala
I
Palenqué
Tikál
Mitla
C
Seibal
O
Quirigua
Copan
Pacific Ocean

From Parlours to Pyramids

'... An inherent propensity to wander ...'

> An inherent propensity to wander, and, not improbably, some slight wish to secure a share in the golden prospects held out to all persons emigrating to the Australian Colonies, induced me, once more to encounter the perils of the deep, and to bid adieu, for a time, to those luxuries and comforts so much prized by all who love a life of tranquility.
> [Breton, Lieut., 1834]

With minor alterations, this could have been written by Adela Breton herself. However, the quote is from the preface of a book by her father, who seems to have transmitted this 'inherent propensity to wander' to his daughter. In 1910, when she was sixty years old, she wrote:

> As you see, I am safely started on the S. American trip. After looking forward to it for so many years (ever since I was 12 years old) I feared something might prevent ...
> [AB to Tozzer, 29 April 1910 PM]

Her father's career was with the Royal Navy, and he had travelled extensively in the Far East, always bringing home curios. His interest in archaeology was also transmitted to Adela:

> I may tell you that I have been travelling & studying in Mexico for the last 12 years, & all my life have been learning archaeology as my Father was much interested in it.
> [AB to Quick, 30 January 1905 BCM]

William Breton married Elizabeth d'Arch when he was forty-five. Five years later, Adela Catherine Breton was born, on 31 December 1849, in England. Eighteen months later her brother, Harry d'Arch Breton, was born (Fig.1). By this time, the Bretons had settled in Bath, at 15 Camden Crescent. Miss Breton was to make this her base throughout her travels.

Adela Breton's father was one of ten children, many of whom as adults served in the military or married military officers. References to cousins and relations occur in her letters, and one has the impression that the family was congenial.

In later letters Adela referred to family trips on the continent when she was growing up, but whether the family travelled more extensively than that is not known. Her grandfather was referred to as Peter Breton 'of Jamaica', and there may have been visits to see him.

We do not know much about Adela Breton's art training and schooling. Art had a definite place in a young woman's education in the Victorian era. Young women

1 Family portrait of Adela Breton with her mother Elizabeth d'Arch Breton (1820-1874), her father Commander William Breton (1799-1889) and her father's twin brother, General Henry Breton (1799-1887). Her brother Harry and the General's daughter Eliza are missing from the portrait. Ea 11509

were taught by drawing masters, and schools or seminaries for young ladies featured art in their curricula. By this time women were making lives for themselves in many of the arts, and it was more or less accepted that women could earn money by their writing. Women artists, although still faced with many barriers, were not the rarities they had been in the earlier part of the century.

It is not known just when Miss Breton began her travels to the New World. It may have been soon after the death of her father, in 1887. (Her mother had died in 1874, the same year Harry married).

In 1894 she went to Mexico and travelled extensively through the country. She carried a sketchbook, using it for pencil studies or small sketches, dating the drawings and identifying the location, providing us with some information about her travels in those years (Pls.48-50).

These experiences in Mexico may have led her to contact Alfred Percival Maudslay, a noted British archaeologist who had worked throughout the Maya region. She reputedly asked him if there was some work she could do in Mexico, and he replied that she might travel to Chichén Itzá in the Yucatán peninsula and verify the accuracy of some of his drawings. She might also make copies of some of the paintings and bas reliefs that were already showing serious wear and damage from exposure.

This was a turning point in her life. In 1900 she went to Chichén Itzá, and from then until her death in 1923 she travelled widely in Central and South America, Egypt, Australia, Japan and Fiji. Altogether, between 1900 and 1908 she was to make thirteen trips to Mexico.

Although her home was still in Camden Crescent, Bath, she lived there only for short intervals.

> If you could see the chaos into which my house has drifted in the last 12 years that I have been almost entirely absent ...
> [AB to Tozzer, 7 August 1921 PM]

She became increasingly drawn into her Americanist work. Her circle of colleagues grew, and the range of her work expanded. She began to publish some of her work, and she was an active participant at many professional meetings.

Despite her travels and growing professional reputation, she and Harry Breton seemed to have remained close. In 1901 his wife died, and in 1903 his only daughter also died. On both occasions, Miss Breton went to help him.

> The life here (England) kills me, but I do not like to leave my brother.
> [AB to Tozzer, 18 November 1903 PM]

As the years progressed, her health became of more concern to her. She often wrote of the killing winters in England, particularly in Bath, with their chill and damp. Increasingly, arthritis became a problem and interfered with her work.

> The dry heat when I went to Yucatan did my hands & arms great good, & I was able to draw without the great pain & difficulty of the previous 18 months, but now they are getting bad again.
> [AB to Putnam, 21 July 1907 HUA]

She spent several winters in eastern Canada, enjoying the dry cold and sunshine; her health was always uncertain, however, and she suffered at least one serious fall.

In 1920 she returned to Bath, where she continued to work, copying manuscripts and working on her father's collection of South Seas material. In 1922, although in poor health, she sailed to Rio de Janiero to attend a conference. After visiting South America, Adela planned to travel to Canada, and proceed to Portugal before going back to England. Ill-health forced her to stop in Barbados for a time.

> I have been three months at Barbados, ill & incapable all the time ... Send me a line if you can, on the chance of my being here still. I may stay through May.
> [AB to Tozzer, 27 April 1923 PM]

Adela Breton died in Barbados on 13 June 1923. Harry Breton survived her by a year. He died in July 1924, leaving one son.

Chichén Itzá

Adela Breton first went to Chichén Itzá in 1900, when she was fifty. The Yucatán peninsula of Mexico was extremely isolated at the turn of the century, and life, then, at an archaeological site was arduous. She kept a 'diary' while she was at Chichén Itzá, and the entries talk of heat and ticks.

I have been looking through my diaries of Chichen & reviving long buried memories. Food, fever, & suffering from bites of many kinds, occupy a large space in the diaries ... One scarcely knew what one was doing in that struggle to exist & work.
[AB to Tozzer, 22 August 1921 PM]

Pablo Solorio, her guide, was an important part of life at Chichén and her travels in Mexico. Pablo collected artefacts for her, and several times she tried to arrange commissions for him for his work. She was to become concerned at not hearing from him:

I have not heard from Pablo since I left Merida & feel anxious about him as he has such a talent for being unlucky.
[AB to Tozzer, 28 August 1904 PM].

Pablo had died, possibly of yellow fever.

I am sure you will be sorry to hear I have lost my good Pablo. I can hardly bear to think of or realize it yet ... I suppose he must have developed a fever on the steamer & perhaps been taken to the hospital & died without having time to give his address. He had no strength to resist an illness. Oh, Chichen! How much it has cost me ... His poor wife - waiting from day to day ... I warn you against having anything to do with the ruins. Everyone who has, has been unlucky. I did think I might escape, as I was not digging up graves or hidden things. My sister-in-law my niece & now Pablo ... You have no idea what a help he was to me in every way. I should never have done anything without him ... At present I feel completely crushed by this catastrophe ... Enjoy your home while you have it - one so takes one's home & one's parents for granted, - until they are gone.
[AB to Tozzer, 20 September 1904 PM]

She remembered and spoke of Pablo all her life. In a letter she wrote on 16 April 1912 - the day after the sinking of the Titanic - she said:

Pablo often said the risk of travelling was that one might be involved in the fate prepared for others.
[AB to Tozzer, 16 April 1912 PM].

Chichén was more than heat and ticks and hunger and personal bereavement. She often spoke of Chichén with nostalgia.

It was delicious up there (Upper Temple of the Jaguars) with the fresh air blowing through, & the tall grass outside making music in the wind.
[AB to Tozzer, 4 May 1902 PM]

Spite of garrapatas [ticks], I shall always look back on Chichen days as some of my happiest.
[AB to Tozzer, 9 December 1911 PM]

One of Adela Breton's most enduring contributions are her superb watercolours of Chichén Itzá.

Other archaeological sites in Mexico

Although much of her time in Mexico was concentrated on Chichén Itzá, she travelled to many other archaeological sites and often made sketches of them.

Some of her most famous work was at Acancéh, south west of Chichén Itzá. In 1907, she spent five weeks copying the painted reliefs (Pl.25).

> The new reliefs at Acanceh are thought very interesting. It is extraordinary, both there & at Teotihuacán, to see how buildings have been added to, & covered over, old worked stones used in rebuilding, frescoes painted over former ones ...
> [AB to Putnam, 21 July 1907 HUA]

Today these reliefs have almost completely disappeared, and her watercolours at the City of Bristol Museum are the most comprehensive record which survives.

Aké, a site in the Yucatán, also aroused her interest (Pl.27):

> I was sorry to hear that Chichen is to be subjected to thorough excavation ... The mounds at Ake, I should have thought much more suitable - so many (60 or more) & nothing visible of their interiors.
> [AB to Bowditch, 16 January 1914 PM]

Earlier, travelling along the coast of the Gulf of Mexico into northern Veracruz, she had visited El Tajín (Pls.30–31). This site aroused her curiosity:

> I have just been reading over my letters home from Mexico nearly 20 years ago, when I went to Papantla. No one seemed to care about Mexican antiquities then. I feel sure there is a great deal of importance at Papantla if proper examination could be made - I mean of course at the ruins, which are about 5 miles away from the town. I noted many large mounds dimly visible in the thick forest, & there were a number of stone

2 Pen and ink drawing of the north end of the west side of the Pyramid of the Feathered Serpent at Xochicalco. Ea 8271b

sculptures from the temple on the summit of the pyramid (El Tajin). A very fine carved stela with a human figure, rather in the style of the "palmas".
[AB to Bowditch, 15 June 1914 PM]

In highland Mexico she photographed and drew at Xochicalco (Pl.40 and Fig.2) and sent the drawings and manuscript for display at the Congress of Americanists held in Vienna in 1908. Referring to the drawings, she wrote to her friend Dr Tozzer at the Peabody Museum, Harvard University, 'Perhaps you will think it great rubbish.' [AB to Tozzer not dated PM].

She kept up with the restoration work at the sites - not always approving of the work. After seeing a photograph of the 'restoration' at Xochicalco, she wrote:

Words fail to express my feelings at such an atrocity. I can only say that Batres' [Mexican Inspector of Monuments] cup of iniquities has now overflowed ... Teotihuacan, Mitla & now this, & he still lives! & and has perhaps 10 years more to do worse in.
[AB to Tozzer, 19 January 1911 PM]

Miss Breton became increasingly involved with Meso-American archaeology. Her early publications were centred on her copying, while later articles showed the broader scope of her work.

As her professional orientation expanded, so too, did her acquaintance of other Americanists. She corresponded with several of them; her letters to Tozzer, for instance, cover more than twenty years and reflect a deepening friendship. Tozzer, an early Harvard PhD, trained a generation of students in Middle American archaeology.

She took an interest in the work of Annie Hunter, an artist who copied hieroglyphics for Maudslay. Although Miss Hunter and her sisters did not travel in the field, they earned Miss Breton's respect.

I hope that Miss [Annie] Hunter will be recognized some day as one of the best of pioneer Americanists.
[AB to Tozzer, 25 October 1916 PM]

She also admired Miss Fletcher, a pioneer ethnologist noted for her work among native Americans of North America:

...I have enjoyed spending some quiet evenings with Miss Fletcher. One day she read to me some of the songs in her Hako ceremony ... it will be a great misfortune if she should die without passing on her intimate knowledge of the Indian mind. Send one of your best young men here to sit at her feet.
[AB to Tozzer, 13 May 1916 PM]

A letter from Mr La Flesche told me of Miss Fletcher's sad breakdown. Is she still alive? I shall miss her very much. She was such a warm loyal friend to me & her letters so interesting.
[AB to Tozzer, 27 April 1923 PM]

Adela Breton and Zelia Nuttall, the leading female Americanist from the United States, were acquainted:

She (Mrs Nuttall) knows so much more about those things than anyone else that it is regrettable she should have been diverted to Elizabethan times.
[AB to Tozzer, 8 May 1920 PM]

Miss Breton attended many professional congresses, and she was active in the Congresses of the Americanists. She and Franz Boas, the 'architect' of modern American anthropology, co-edited the journal of the proceedings of the 1912 Congress:

Everything has been left for me to do & think of.It may be a compliment but it means ever so much work & responsibility.
[AB to Bowditch, 22 March 1914 PM].

She became involved in the fortunes of the Le Plongeons, who had worked at Chichén Itzá before her. Although they were now professionally ostracised for their lost continent theories, she had arranged to have money forwarded anonymously to them. For several years she sent $100 a year in semi-annual remittances. The director of the Peabody Museum, F. W. Putnam (and Miss Mead, his assistant) handled the remittances for her. It is not certain when this started, but by 1906 she was a little weary of the arrangement.

I should be sorry to have to give up the le Plongeons, tho' I fear they will wear out my patience as they seem to have that of their other well wishers. Perhaps when the January remittance comes they might be told they will only get it once a year afterward instead of twice. I am sure she guesses that I send her money, as I get a letter about once a month, asking after my health & a wail over their circumstances. Such a waste of 5 cents stamps!
[AB to Mead, 31 July 1906 HUA]

...send (the remittance) only on January 1st. I did not intend to go on for ever with the allowance. When I began, I supposed they were in temporary difficulties - one always has fresh objects of necessity turning up ...
[AB to Putnam, 21 July 1907 HUA]

She cut back the remittance to $50 a year. After Mr Le Plongeon's death, she reflected on his lot:

Poor man! why are some people accepted & not others? Dr. Seler often makes mistakes, & changes his opinions, but he founds a school & is thought a shining light ... I will continue it [the remittance] for the present ... I hope the withdrawal of $50 did not make it really more difficult for them. [She relates that she had felt the need to economise because she was having to help out a relation.]
[AB to Mead, 15 February 1909 HUA]

One of her most interesting acquaintanceships - and certainly the most problematic - was Edward Thompson, United States Consul to the Yucatán. His diplomatic duties took second place to his archaeological interests. He was in charge of Chichén Itzá while Miss Breton worked there, and they did not get along.

[Tozzer had sent her a supply of drawing paper from Mérida, but Thompson at Chichén Itzá did not give it to her for three weeks.]

It was rather amusing, & very annoying, to stay on by main force as it were, against their will [Thompsons]. But my work became more important as I went on, & I could not be driven away.
[AB to Tozzer, 9 May 1903 PM]

It is lucky you have not wanted to stay at Chichen yet as there seems to be absolutely no place this year - Mr. T. has managed very cleverly to keep everyone out.
[AB to Tozzer, 31 March 1904 PM]

There was another side - Thompson's - to these difficulties.

Miss Breton is here and I gather from what the tourists say who went with her to Uxmal she's a ... tartar. They say she complained all the way out all the time while she was there and all the way back. In fact a New York gentleman, Mr Stebbins, who owns Eagle Harbor, Maine, and his sister say that she made life a burden to them on the trip. According to her ideas everyone was leagued against her, even to her volan driver to make her trip unpleasant for her. Well, I fussed around and made arrangements for her to get to Chichen as well and comfortable as possible and she went. I told her before she went that the authorities are now very strict on the matter of working in the ruins and that to make things all right she should have had a permit from the authorities to do her class of work among the Yucatan ruins. She stated however that if necessary Maudslay would have obtained one for her. Of course I had nothing more to say. I only cautioned her to be careful in treating with the Inspector and keep on his right side in order to make things as easy as possible for her. Yesterday I got a letter in which she, after bewailing her lot states that because of some action of hers or because of something she did or tried to do, I don't exactly understand what from her letter, the Inspector has forbidden her permission to even sketch.
[Thompson to Putnam, 3 March 1900 HUA]

The 'incident' ended with Adela being served with an injunction. She then promised to conform with the laws, the injunction was relaxed, and she was permitted to sketch and draw. Matters between Thompson and Adela did not improve very much, however.

Miss Breton returned from Chichen today I understand. To tell the honest truth she's a nuisance. She is a ladylike person but full of whims, complaints and prejudices. Were she to keep her servant to herself and to her own work, it would not be so bad, but "Pablo" her native servant, is, I think at her instigation, constantly prying around where I am working. Do the best I could I couldn't keep him away unless I used the kicking hint. I didn't care to do this and preferred to leave the search for and excavation of certain sepulchres for a later date when no meddlers are on hand.

To my horror I found out the day I left Chichen that she proposes to return to Chichen shortly for another period of time. She certainly is an artist as regards landscapes at least and she has made one painting in the intervals of her work for Maudslay that is really very nice. She brought out the artistic points of the "Nunnery" in a wonderful manner.
[Thompson to Putnam, 5 April 1900 HUA]

By July, Thompson must have been feeling more moderate.

> I am glad Miss Breton had pleasant remembrances of her visit to Chichen. We tried to do what we could to make her stay as pleasant as possible but I was not at all sure whether my efforts were successful or not. She has a very peculiar character but I think that she is one of those persons that improve as one knows them better. She most certainly is a true artist.
> [Thompson to Putnam, 29 July 1900 HUA]

Bowditch and Putnam, of the Peabody Museum, concerned about 'their' project at Chichén Itzá, took note of the difficulties between Adela and Thompson.

> I note what you say about Miss Breton and I certainly hope that she will be willing to leave her drawings with us. We must try to keep on better terms with her than Thompson is though I heartily sympathize with him in having such an unsatisfactory old soul bothering him in his work.
> [Bowditch to Putnam, 6 August 1902 HUA]

The Peabody Museum did receive a number of fine reduced-scale watercolours of the Chichén Itzá fresco. Full scale drawings, in addition to a set of reduced scale, were bequeathed to the City of Bristol Museum.

Adela Breton's attitude to her work

A major aspect of Miss Breton's work was the copying and colouring of relief carvings, wall paintings, artefacts and manuscripts. She took an academic approach, and was extremely concerned about the accuracy of what she did: she saw her job as copying exactly what was there, not drawing in an interpretive manner. It was painstaking work.

Her comments about - and the underlying worry with - the accuracy of the figures and the colour, the methods of reproducing and copying, and even how one looked at the frescos, sculptures, and reliefs, all spoke of the difficulty of the work.

> I may say that the South West piece of fresco [at Chichén Itzá] I copied 13 times, always correcting it carefully. In that way one trains eye & hand.
> [AB to Tozzer, 22 August 1921 PM]

> I feel strongly that the only satisfactory way to record those sculptures, [North end of Ball Court, Fig.3] is to have good photos. & go over them on the spot, putting in day by day the details as one gradually sees them.
> [AB to Tozzer, 18 June 1904 PM]

Referring to drawings to be published:

> Making drawings of them would require not modern artistic skill, but the very different capacity of seeing them as ancient Americans did.
> [AB to Tozzer, 18 September 1921 PM]

While she was at the sites she sketched and copied extensively. Making additional copies later was difficult, and she tried various aids. Commenting on photography she wrote:

North Building, Ball Court, Chichén Itzá.

3 Pen and ink drawing of the figure from the base of the eastern column of the North Building of the Ball Court, Chichén Itzá, showing two recumbent figures, elaborately dressed, holding up a serpent (Breton 1917). Ea 8192f

When I wanted to reproduce my full size tracings of the Chichen frescoes, I thought they could easily be photographed to quarter scale, & had two large pieces done, but they gave me immense trouble because they were never quite right & did not fit, besides being dim in places. Drawing to scale was the only right method.
[AB to Bowditch, 13 February 1916 PM]

Many of her letters discussed in detail the problems of scale and accuracy.

I had just finished colouring the photos. to send to you ... I do not consider them fit for reproduction, as they do not give the light effect of the original. It is almost impossible with coloured photos. I was trying experiments in copying, & feel sure the only satisfactory way is to make careful full-size outlines from my rough copies, & have them reduced & then coloured ...
[AB to Putnam, 16 October 1904 HUA]

The drawing [of the Chichén Itzá fresco she was doing for Peabody] to 1/4 scale gets on very slowly in these twilight days, & when the outline is done I shall have to trace it, redraw & colour it, which will be at least a month's work ... Drawing in 1/32 of an inch & correcting to 1/64 is very trying to brain & nerves as well as to eyes & hand, & I have now had 18 months of it.
[AB to Mead, 28 December 1906 HUA]

Colour was a recurring theme:

In the second copy (also done from my original copy) [the Chichén Itzá fresco] I left out the green on one or two of the lower figures because I did not feel sure they were intended to be green. It looked more like the ground color, which had become very dark.
[AB to Tozzer, 25 February 1916 PM]

An occasional small bit of colour might be left out & I know by experience how many times one has to go over those complicated things to make sure that every scrap of colour is in.
[AB to Bowditch, 16 February 1916 PM]

At one point she even utilised outside help.

> I am going to try my hand on the door jamb figures ... but fear my painting days will soon be over.
> [AB to Tozzer, 26 April 1906 PM]

> My brother has only just begun the second of the door post figures, as, altho' he is an expert draughtsman & works several hours a day, they take an immense time ... I fear his views as to their value or rather of my drawings from them would not suit the Peabody.
> [AB to Mead, 28 December 1906 HUA]

Repeatedly in her letters she referred to the physical difficulty of making the copies and reproductions, and the pressure on her to do more:

> But really, for this copying of codices - in fact all Americanist work, it is better not to try to work continuously. It is most trying to one's eyes & I have not yet recovered from copying the "Maguey Map" (Pl.41) for Mr Maudslay in Mexico in 1908.
> [AB to Bowditch, 22 January 1916 PM]

The demand for her work grew, and she frequently referred to the prospect of several years' work ahead of her. She made distinctions between commissions and her own research interests.

> I want very much to get on with my own work & see about publishing my fresco copies & the Acanceh reliefs, & then do some more field work before I am too old. The years pass so quickly.
> [AB to Bowditch, 17 December 1913 PM]

As she became involved in copying manuscripts, maps and codices, she became caught up in languages. At one point she cited the need for intimate knowledge of a language to help guard against mistakes and inaccuracies creeping into the work.

She knew Spanish and could manage German, although she did not particularly like that language. Her repertoire expanded to include some Mayan languages:

> As I have really done a lot of work on the Kekchi & Pokomchi, I would suggest that you should take up something else.The Tzaldal vocabularies ... are most interesting & valuable ...
> [AB to Tozzer, 11 May 1917 PM]

She was enthusiastic about the Pokonchi & Cholti languages; Yucatán Maya was a different story, however:

> I do not feel that I shall ever make much headway myself with Maya, tho' of course one comes to recognize words & expressions.
> [AB to Tozzer, 4 September 1919 PM]

Her scholarship, both as a transcriber and as a student of languages, governed much of her life. She often mentioned how important it was to have work. In a letter to

Miss Mead she agreed that, '...it is very nice "to have a definite object in life".' [AB to Mead, 26 March 1909 HUA].

Mexico ... and Miss Breton

Of all the many countries she visited, Mexico seemed to have earned a special place in Adela Breton's affections:

> After so many years of going to Mexico about this time, it seems quite strange to be unable to put oneself in the train ... 13 times I went into Mexico.
> [AB to Tozzer, 7 March 1917 PM]

> It is strange in life, how things come to an end. Never to have gone back since 1908! to Mexico.
> [AB to Tozzer, 22 August 1921 PM]

> I feel very thankful to have had all these long journeys & voyages without serious difficulties, & now should like to do just a little more if I can & while I can. The years run away so & and the night cometh.
> [AB to Tozzer, 2 December 1914 PM]

Mary McVicker

British Contributions to Maya Archaeology: Adela Breton's paintings of Acancéh

During the first decades following Mexico's independence from Spain in 1821, when Europeans were no longer shut out from visiting the new republic, a wealth of reports of the country's condition was published. One of the first British travellers, William Bullock, who spent six months in the country, issued a detailed account of his travels and also described some of the ancient monuments (Bullock 1823). With the permission of the local authorities he procured a considerable number of Aztec stone and clay statues.He made plaster models of the two pyramids at Teotihuacán, acquired several indigenous manuscripts and hieroglyphic documents, and gave an account of newly discovered monuments that turned up during construction work in Mexico City. His collection of originals and casts - including the Aztec Calendar Stone and a 'sacrificial stone' (probably the Stone of Tizoc) - was exhibited in the Egyptian Hall in Piccadilly, London, built to house his museum of 'curiosities'.

The second half of the nineteenth century witnessed an intensive investigation of the natural resources and sociological conditions in Mexico and British travellers contributed substantially to the archaeological exploration of ancient Maya ruins that lay hidden in the rain forest.

The first British archaeological expedition to the ancient city of Palenque, in the state of Chiapas, departed from British Honduras in 1839. It was led by John Herbert Caddy, then a lieutenant in the Royal Artillery, and Patrick Walker, an official in 'the Settlement' as it used to be called. Their report has been published in its complete form by David M Pendergast (1967) who was able to discover Walker's diary and related documents, presumed to be lost, in the Colonial Office archives. Unfortunately, the corresponding paintings had disappeared. The Walker-Caddy expedition travelled laboriously from the town of Belize to Palenque in eighteen days, a journey that can now be accomplished in three hours.

By coincidence, also in 1839, another expedition to Chiapas, Yucatán and Central America was organized by John L Stephens. His Incidents of Travel (1841 and 1843) were superbly illustrated by the London-born architect Frederick Catherwood (1799-1854). His twenty-five fine colour plates were published in 1844 and reproduced in 1964 and their beauty and painstaking accuracy are still much admired (Carmichael 1973).

As noted by Eduard Seler (1849-1922), the German archaeologist who travelled extensively in Mexico and Guatemala, mostly on foot or on horseback, European readers were fascinated by Stephens' and Catherwood's description and drawings of Copán. When the noted British archaeologist Alfred P. Maudslay (1850-1931) visited Copán briefly in 1881 he was determined to return to make a more thorough investigation of the ruins. His explorations at Copán and other archaeological sites, were published at length in the Archaeology volumes of *Biologia Centrali Americana* (Maudslay 1889 - 1902).

Maudslay, like Bullock sixty years earlier, made moulds (by means of paper squeezes) of the inscriptions, and plaster copies of entire monuments which are now in the British Museum (British Museum 1923). His researches inaugurated the first intensive study of Maya ruins and ranged from Chichén Itzá in the north to Copán (Honduras) and from Tikal in Guatemala to Palenque in the west.

Archival research also resulted in important British publications. Soon after Cortés arrived in Veracruz in 1519 the Aztec emperor sent him valuable presents of gold ornaments, inlaid wood carvings, shields with mosaic featherwork, and pottery. It is of particular significance, for scholarly research, that among these gifts were the pictorial manuscripts (codices) which contained ritual-calendric almanacs used by the priests for prognostication. These objects were carefully recorded by the Spaniards before they were sent to Charles V and were greatly admired when they were exhibited in Europe. A list of one shipment specified how the treasure should be distributed among those personalities - secular and ecclesiastical - who maintained close relations with the Hapsburg empire. For this reason a considerable number of Pre-Hispanic objects eventually found their way into various European museums. There are at least eight important pictorial manuscripts in British libraries and museums which reached England in various circumstances (See Appendix).

To make the widely dispersed codices available for study, Edward King, Viscount Kingsborough (1795-1837), commissioned the artist Augustine Aglio who painstakingly copied the manuscripts. Kingsborough published his valuable sources, including the Maya Codex Dresdensis, in nine elegant volumes (the pages measure 54 x 36cm) in *Antiquities of Mexico* (1831). A colour reprint in reduced size by the Mexican Government, with commentaries in Spanish, appeared in 1964 (Kingsborough 1964). Although many of these codices have recently been faithfully reproduced with introductory notes, by the Akademische Druck- und Verlagsanstalt in Graz, Austria, the Kingsborough edition is still valuable for comparisons inasmuch as some details have, in time, been obliterated in the originals.

It is against this background of British contributions to Maya studies that we focus our attention on Adela Breton, who is being honoured by this exhibition.

An early publication by Miss Breton (1903) does not relate to Maya archaeology but to the figural art of West Mexico. It is an account of a rich mortuary offering of over twenty large ceramic figures discovered in 1896 in a large mound some ten miles north of Etzatlán, Jalisco(Pls.32-34). She included drawings of three of these figures and of some shell ornaments. Inasmuch as virtually all West Mexican Shaft Tomb figures are derived from looted tombs and are therefore of unspecified provenance, Breton's article is important because it indicates the precise location of the find and the *in situ* associations of two well-known types of Jalisco figures (Meighan and Nicholson 1970: 19).

Miss Breton travelled frequently to Mexico between 1894 and 1907, where she became acquainted with Maya ruins in Yucatán. Alfred Maudslay, who appreciated her artistic talent, suggested to her that she copy the murals and sculptures at Chichén

Itzá. This she accomplished so successfully that she earned the praise of the then dean of American archaeologists, Professor Alfred Tozzer, who was the first to offer formal instruction in Middle American archaeology at Harvard.

About 1907, while Adela Breton was in Yucatán, news reached her of the discovery of mural paintings on the stucco façade of a 'palace' at Acancéh, some 25km south east of Mérida. A small town had been built upon the Pre-Hispanic site, of which only two major structures remain today, a pyramid once decorated with large stucco masks and the 'Palace of the Stuccoes'. The latter is of particular interest because the frieze on the upper vault is decorated in a unique manner with mythological animals in a series of panels (Pl.25). The palace mound suffered severe damage from being used as a quarry. Almost all of the local Colonial period buildings, including the church at Acancéh, were built of stones taken from Pre-Hispanic structures, which turned the latter into shapeless mounds. Later, on the occasion of the centenary celebration of Mexico's independence in 1911, large quantities of stones were taken for building the village plaza. As a result of this ongoing destruction the stucco frieze became exposed.

When Eduard Seler and his wife visited Acancéh in 1907 both the eastern and western corners of the building had been destroyed and they observed further damage on their second visit in 1911. Seler made a drawing of the reliefs which, at that time, were for the most part in good condition. His wife took photographs in 1907 and 1911. Teobert Maler, the Austrian archaeologist, known for his superb photographs of Maya ruins in Guatemala, photographed the frieze in 1908.

Seler published a detailed iconographic study of the frieze (Fig.4) in German and included excellent line drawings (Seler 1915a). In his monograph he states:

> Adela Breton, the keenly interested and indefatigable researcher laboriously copied the splendid frescos of the Temple of the Jaguars and the Shields at Chichén Itzá, in lifesize and in its natural colours, and spent some months in 1907 copying the stucco façade at Acancéh in colour and in natural size. It is very much to be desired that Miss Breton be given the opportunity to publish one or the other paintings in adequate and dignified form.
> [Seler 1915a: 403, transl. HvW]

Unfortunately, this wish has so far not been fulfilled. [Prohibitive reproduction costs enabled me to publish only one segment of Adela Breton's paintings on the cover of my recent monograph (von Winning 1985)].

4 Front elevation of the Palace of the Stuccoes at Acancéh, showing the position of the stucco frieze, after Seler and Marquina (1951).

Had it not been for Miss Breton's diligent and patient endeavours to trace and colour her copies of the frescos shortly after they had come to light in 1907, we would have no knowledge of the original appearance of the frieze. Seler observed (Seler 1915a: 392) that the stucco frieze displayed brilliant ('leuchtend') colours against a red background when he saw it, and this is evident in Breton's copies. Today the reliefs are in a deplorable condition and only scant traces of the polychromy remain.

[See Appendix for information concerning Pre-Hispanic and Post-Conquest pictorial manuscripts in British collections.]

5 Outline tracing of the wall painting on south end of west wall of the inner chamber, Upper Temple of the Jaguars, at Chichén Itzá, showing a scene after a battle, see Cat.No 25. Ea 8151a

Dr Hasso von Winning

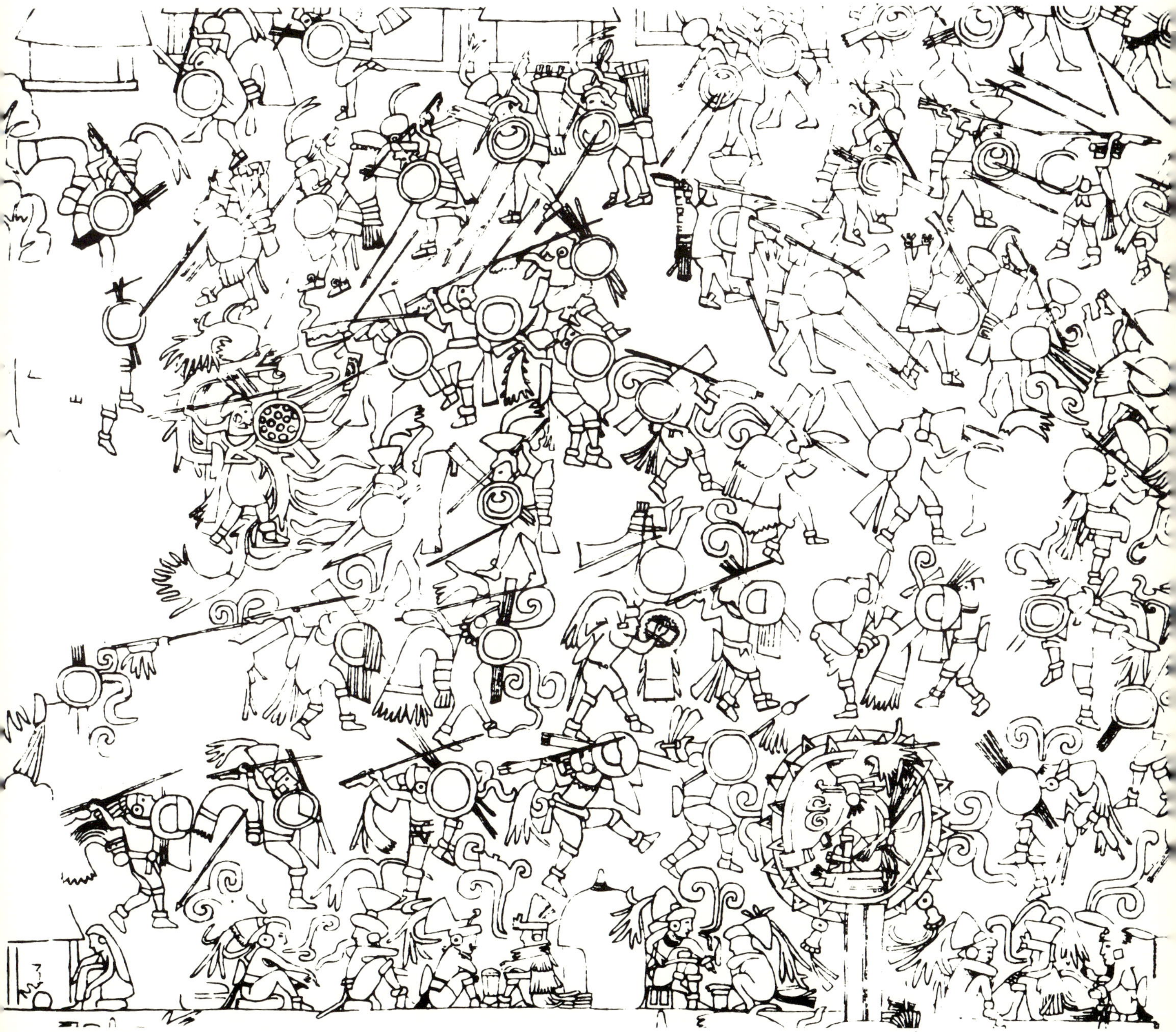

Adela Breton at Teotihuacán

When, on 15 February 1894, Adela Breton sat on the overgrown Pyramid of the Moon at the immense site of Teotihuacán some 50km to the north-east of Mexico City and sketched the scene below her (Fig.6), she could not have known that she was soon to make the most complete record that exists of a unique set of frescos less than three kilometres to the south of where she sat. It was not until the following May that Sr José María Barrios, a land-owning Indian in the village of San Sebastian Teotihuacán, uncovered the remains of an ancient building while foraging for stone on his property. Its walls, less than a metre high, bore vestiges of elaborate mural paintings. This was the structure known as Teopancaxco which Dr Antonio Peñafiel, the Mexican scholar, who was the first to write extensively about Teotihuacán, called a corruption of Teopancalco, 'Place of the Temple Dwellings', though we cannot know if that bears any relation to what the ancient Teotihuacanos called it.

Dr Peñafiel described the paintings as badly 'mutilated' and, recognising that further deterioration was almost inevitable despite the rudimentary shelter built to protect some of them, made coloured tracings of the four main mural fragments. Sepia versions of most of these tracings were included in his 1900 book on Teotihuacán (Peñafiel 1900). They formed the basis for the illustrations of the murals in the study of the site published by the eminent German scholar, Eduard Seler, in 1915 (Seler 1915b). In addition, Seler used an illustration of one of the Teopancaxco figures which he attributed to Miss Adela Breton, saying that she also had made copies of the other murals at the site. Contrasting these tracings with the doubtful accuracy of the only copies of the murals in Teotihuacán's Temple of Agriculture, which had by then deteriorated beyond recognition, he commended Peñafiel and Breton as reliable observers whose tracings had rescued the Teopancaxco murals 'for all future time for scientific study' (Seler 1915b: 414).

This handsome tribute by the foremost Meso-Americanist of his time has been only partially justified by developments in this century. Peñafiel's copies are widely known in their black and white published version but his original colour tracings were not published. Adela Breton's copies, more complete than those of Peñafiel and pristine in their colours, have never been reproduced apart from the single line drawing in Seler (Seler 1915b: Abb.8). As for the frescos themselves, a visit to Teopancaxco reveals the accuracy of Peñafiel's melancholy prediction that the vagaries of the weather would soon destroy the surviving vestiges. Recent efforts at conservation and the construction of a new shelter have saved a much faded, left lower portion of the main mural known as 'The Pulque Priests', but little else remains. For these reasons the copies made by Adela Breton are of prime importance and this exhibition is a welcome means for making them known to scholars and a wider audience.

Peñafiel made his tracings very soon after the discovery of the Teopancaxco murals and Adela Breton may have become aware of them through his work. The only one of her watercolours to bear a date - March 1895 - is a rough miniature (Ea 8361) of the central motif and right-hand figure of the Pulque Priests mural. Possibly, like a couple of her other miniature sketches, it was copied from a Peñafiel photograph. We have evidence for this not only in a reference in Seler (Seler 1915b: 416) to her use of this technique but also in the brief but very informative comments that Adela Breton made on almost all her copies. In several cases she refers to Peñafiel, either stating explicitly that her sketch was 'after Peñafiel', or noting that, in comparing Peñafiel with the original, he had included some feature not evident to her. This indicates very clearly, as does the evidence of the copies themselves, that Peñafiel was first in the field at Teopancaxco. This is not, however, of much significance since it is certain that Adela Breton traced her major copies direct from the original frescos and that even some of her minor sketches, though perhaps copied in outline from Peñafiel, were coloured directly from the originals.

More importantly Adela Breton made the most comprehensive record of the murals of Teopancaxco. Her re-creation of the colours of the murals is unsurpassed compared with the few colour reproductions available and thus constitutes an irreplaceable memorial of the now destroyed masterpieces. The accuracy and nuance of detail in her work supplements that of others who copied the same originals.

An unexpected bonus in the Breton legacy to the City of Bristol Museum is a small sketch plan of Teopancaxco on the reverse of her watercolour of a priestly figure (Ea 8363, see below). This plan (Fig.7) is particularly valuable because it identifies the location of the murals, thus resolving most of the problems that have arisen due to the rather imprecise way in which other copyists have referred to the location of the

6 Pen and ink sketch of the Avenue of the Dead at Teotihuacán, drawn from the Pyramid of the Moon. Date 15.2.94. Ea 8372

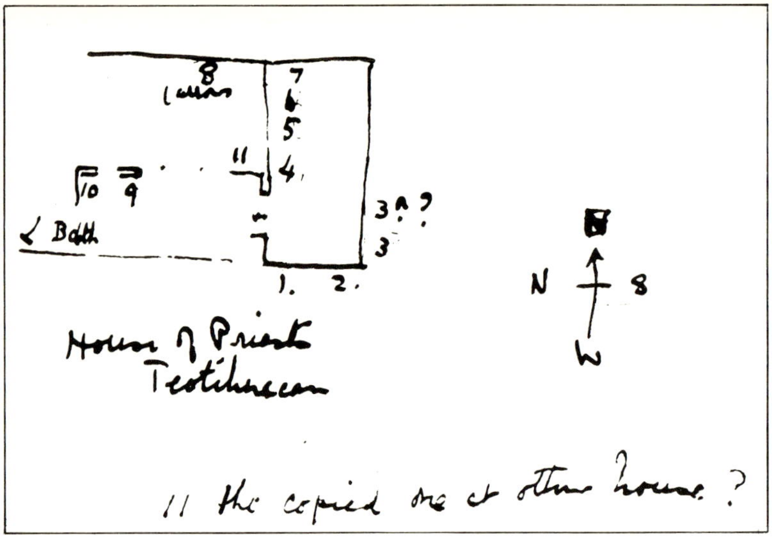

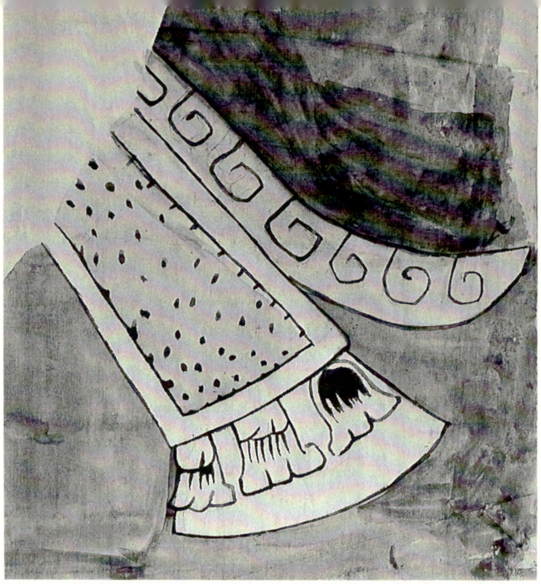

originals. It is important to note that Adela Breton first indicated the north correctly on her plan but then changed this by rotating the compass points 90 degrees anticlockwise, so that they and, more significantly, the notations on her copies, must be corrected. This means that south must be understood when she refers to west, and so forth.

The best known and best preserved murals at Teopancaxco were located in what was called the inner chamber, perhaps because it was roofed over from time to time whereas the rooms immediately to the west have, since their discovery, always been exposed to the elements. The most complete mural is on the south wall and depicts two priestly figures on either side of a central shrine-like motif; it is commonly called 'The Pulque Priests' mural (Pl.22), although a better title might be simply 'Worship' (nos 1 and 2 in Fig.7). Adela Breton's copies of this painting are not only the most complete record we have of it but are also a unique example of the way in which she went about making her tracings of major murals.

First, she made a couple of rough sketches which, it is not unreasonable to assume, preceded her more finished work. The full-size reproduction of the entire mural was copied onto a roll of friable paper of a brownish tone some three metres long (Ea 8359). On this she traced, in red, the outline of the main details of the mural. These outlines were then carefully followed on the reverse of the tracing paper with a soft black pencil or charcoal. Finally, the red outlines on the front of the paper were gone over, this time in black, transferring the original tracing onto a roll of drafting paper for colouring - Adela Breton's finished watercolour of the mural (Ea 8360) coincides exactly with the tracing. We may therefore assume that this watercolour is as faithful a copy as she could make of the mural in its state at that time.

This is of some interest because her coloured copy differs in several ways from that made by Peñafiel. Some minor differences are attributable to deterioration of the mural between the time the two copies were made. Others seem to reflect the somewhat more cursive style employed by Adela Breton in, for example, the drawing of the figures' eyes and headdresses. It is not possible, given the scant remains of the mural today, to determine which copy is the more faithful in these small details. There are, however, two more material discrepancies in the copies and here the balance of the

7 (left) Sketch plan of Casa de Barrios at Teopancaxco, showing position of mural paintings, after Breton. Ea 8363
8 (right) Watercolour of a libation from east wall of Casa de Barrios at Teopancaxco, showing the libation with appended flowers. Ea 8364e

evidence tends to favour Adela Breton. First, she shows three flower blossoms hanging below the libation pouring from the hand of the figure on the left. These are similar to the flowers affixed to the sound scrolls emanating from the mouths of the two figures and, although they are missing from the Peñafiel copy, it is unlikely that she could have imagined this detail. There is some corroborative evidence that other libations in the inner chamber originally also had pendant flowers, since destroyed by the ravages of time.

In his 1915 work, Seler (1915b: 417) states that both the east and west walls of the inner chamber bore figures similar to those on the south wall and that these were depicted, in procession, facing towards the south. He adds that on the east wall there were only very indistinct traces of these figures, copies of which were unknown previously. However, among the watercolours in the Breton collection there are three fragments of which two, although unnumbered, can be assigned to the east wall (no. 3 and no. 3? in Fig.7) on the basis of Adela Breton's notations and circumstantial evidence. The first, (Ea 8364b) is part of a headdress from the most southerly of the east wall figures. The second, (Ea 8364e) is the complete libation and part of the ceremonial bag of the second figure (Fig.8), the most interesting aspect of which is three appended flowers, evidently well preserved at the time she painted them. Whether the flowers existed or not may appear a minor detail but does, in fact, affect the interpretation of the entire decorative scheme of the inner chamber. Seler has, for example, suggested (Seler 1915b: 416) that the presence of flowers would indicate that the libations consisted of *pulque*, with very different implications to a water libation or the scattering of seeds.

Another significant difference between the Peñafiel and Breton versions of the south wall mural is that the latter shows a second band of flowers and shells in the right-hand border. This is probably more easily explained than the disparity in the libations. Seler, writing about two decades after the copies had been made (Seler 1915b: 417), said that there were floral borders, still well preserved at that time, to the south of the doorway, on the west wall. The rest of the west wall mural, consisting of three processional figures and a symbolic motif, lay to the north of the doorway. It would therefore seem that Adela Breton included the detached west wall border in her copy of the south wall mural. This is confirmed by the dimensions of the several copies: Peñafiel's version is 2.65 metres wide, as is Adela Breton's without the second border band; whereas the width with it is 2.80 metres.

Peñafiel seems not to have made a full-size copy of the whole painting of the west wall but rather to have traced its various elements separately. Adela Breton, on the other hand, has left us a version in which the three figures and the symbol are traced in their original relationship to each other (Ea 8364d with Ea 8364a superimposed). Regrettably, the image of the symbol had deteriorated seriously by the time she made her copy but we are fortunate to have what is almost certainly a tracing of this motif from Peñafiel although he does not present it in the context of the west wall.

The murals of the outer chamber, never protected from the elements, have vanished but we can deduce the decorative scheme from the notations on Adela Breton's copies and sketch map. The walls of the southern half of the chamber bore a procession of priestly figures (nos. 9 and 10 in Fig.7) while images of armed men, also in procession, decorated those of the northern half (nos. 8 and 11 in Fig.7). Both Peñafiel and Breton copied these murals. Their priestly figures are identical, Breton having made a small watercolour sketch (Ea 8363) and what is probably a full-size watercolour tracing (Pl.23; Ea 8362).

The situation with regard to the armed figures is less certain. Both artists made similar full-size tracings of a fragment of one of these figures of which no more than three *atlatl* darts and a shield had survived (no. 8 in Fig.7). They also copied a complete figure but their versions differ significantly in presentation and in the rendering of the headdress. Peñafiel's full scale tracing was, he wrote, made from an *in situ* original. Adela Breton made only a small sketch (Ea 8265). She describes this as 'from Peñafiel' and as having been coloured from a copy of the original on a thick piece of stucco cut from an ancient wall and located in a house some distance from Teopancaxco (Pl.24). This reference to Peñafiel is difficult to reconcile with the differences in the headdress depiction. Either Adela Breton meant no more than that he had copied a similar figure, or she modified his version to conform to the stucco fragment which was later transferred to the Teotihuacán Regional Museum and of which her sketch is a faithful copy.

Adela Breton's work at Teopancaxco leaves us a remarkable record of a unique set of Pre-Columbian paintings: it sets a standard against which to assess the other extant copies and offers evidence which helps to illuminate a number of problems of concern to those with both a specialist and a general interest in the art of Teotihuacán.

Dr James Langley

Adela Breton in Yucatán

Adela Breton travelled and sketched widely throughout Mexico, but her greatest accomplishment was undoubtedly her work at the Maya cities of Chichén Itzá and Acancéh, both in Yucatán. The former dominated the Maya area - and perhaps much of Meso-America - during the Terminal Classic and Early Post-Classic periods (c. AD 800 to 1100), while Acancéh, a more modest and less-known site 25km south-east of the modern city of Mérida, dates largely from the late Pre-Classic to the Late Classic (c. 300 BC to post AD 850). At both places Miss Breton spent weeks meticulously recording buildings, architectural and free-standing monumental sculpture, mural paintings, and also smaller objects, many of which have since been lost to time and the elements.

She provided a summary of her activities at Chichén Itzá to Alfred M. Tozzer, who lived in the hut next to hers (Fig.9) for three seasons (Tozzer 1957: 270 and Tozzer to Maxwell, HF 3632), taken from a journal now lost. She also carried a pocket sketch-book in which she made pencil studies and colour sketches, named and dated - 'a diary without words' (Stanton, HF 7706). A series of these sketch-books is housed in the City of Bristol Museum. Adela Breton published relatively little about her work, mostly limiting herself to descriptions of her methods of recording and the monuments themselves (Breton 1906a; 1908; 1912; 1917). Other scholars of her generation, however, often relied on her drawings for their own interpretations (for example Seler 1909: Fig. 112), although it is only recently that her watercolours have begun to be reproduced in colour (Coggins 1984; von Winning 1985; V. Miller in press).

What sets Adela Breton apart from her contemporaries is her interest in colour. Lamenting the scanty information left by early explorers regarding colour (Breton 1906a: 167), she set out to record as faithfully as possible the polychrome stone and stucco sculpture and painted walls that once characterised Pre-Columbian buildings. She also noted that even when the carved surface of relief sculpture had disappeared, the colour had sunk deeply into the stone, providing the outline of what had once been there (Breton 1917: 193-194). A cautious draughtsman, however, Miss Breton never attempted to reconstruct what was no longer visible, warning that:

> ...in attempting a reproduction of this kind there must be a tight rein on the imagination, for when the eye has become somewhat accustomed to the style, it is easy to imagine details...
> [Breton 1917: 193]

Furthermore, she recommended making several drawings of the work being copied and working on them independently, comparing the images to reveal obscure details not otherwise visible in order to complete the final drawing (Breton 1917: 194).

9 Photograph of the hacienda *at Chichén Itzá. 'The foreground house is mine. April 1902.' Ea 11101b*

Adela Breton was also an accomplished photographer, using photographs to supplement her own observations in preparation for her drawings. She recommended taking photographs in different lights and enlarging them as a foundation for drawings (Breton 1917: 193). She inked in outlines on photographs (Pl.21) and sometimes coloured them in her attempts to recreate the original appearance of a relief (for example Breton 1917: pls.3 and 4). Although Miss Breton's photographs do illustrate some of her articles, it is unfortunate that only a few are extant in the City of Bristol Museum.

Miss Breton spent several productive seasons at Chichén Itzá (Fig.12) between 1900 and 1907, on one occasion staying for over four months. Her efforts included watercolours of the façade of the annexe to the Monjas complex (Pl.4), the frescos of the Monjas temple, the doorjambs of the Castillo, the lintel of the Akab Dzib, which served at one point as her home, and objects taken fresh from the Cenote of Sacrifice by Edward H. Thompson (Tozzer 1957: 270) (Pl.6). She concentrated her attention, however, on preserving the sculpture and painting of the complex of structures associated with the Great Ballcourt, the largest ballcourt in Meso-America. One task was to photograph and draw the reliefs of its North Building (Breton 1917). Another was to correct Maudslay's drawings of the reliefs in the Lower Temple of the Jaguars, of which casts painted with Miss Breton's hues exist in both the Peabody Museum at Harvard and the University Museum at Philadelphia (Tozzer HF 3262). At the Upper Temple of the Jaguars, she copied the lintel and doorjambs of the inner room as well as the fifteen Atlantean figures and the altar they once supported, all found just outside the chamber. Most important, however, are her reproductions of the now- obliterated frescos of the Upper Temple (Pl.19).

For the murals, Adela Breton used 36 yards (32.92m) of 27 inch-wide (686mm) paper, tracing and then colouring the images (Tozzer 1957: 270). After making lifesize copies of the wall paintings she then reduced them to one quarter of their natural size, filling in details (Fig.10) and (Fig.11). Additional copies of the reduced images were given to the Peabody Museum in Cambridge, Massachusetts and the museum in Quebec City (Tozzer HF 3262). A line-block of part of the scene of the south wall of the Upper Temple of the Jaguars was also done in 1903, with hand-coloured prints taken from the plate (Pl.00). Although Miss Breton (1917: 193) cautioned against taking moulds of reliefs in bad condition, she did make casts of the wooden lintel and doorjambs of the Upper Temple of the Jaguars, correcting the drawings published earlier by Maudslay (1899-1902: vol. III). Harry d'Arch Breton, her brother, made drawings of the jambs from casts that are now in the City of Bristol Museum (Breton to Quick, HF 7705).

Despite considerable scholarly attention, Chichén Itzá remains poorly understood. Debate continues on its chronology, the ethnic identity of its inhabitants, and the nature of its relationship with the contemporaneous central highland Mexican city of Tula. Although the site's centre has been excavated and reconstructed, the major work was completed by the Carnegie Institution of Washington in the 1920s and 1930s, long before the advent of modern archaeological techniques and approaches that might have shed light on many of the unanswered questions about the site.

10 (left) Detail of fresco on the south end of the east wall, Upper Temple of the Jaguars. From the full-scale copy. Ea 8483

11 (right) Detail of fresco on the south end of the east wall, Upper Temple of the Jaguars. From the 1/4 scale copy. Ea 10951

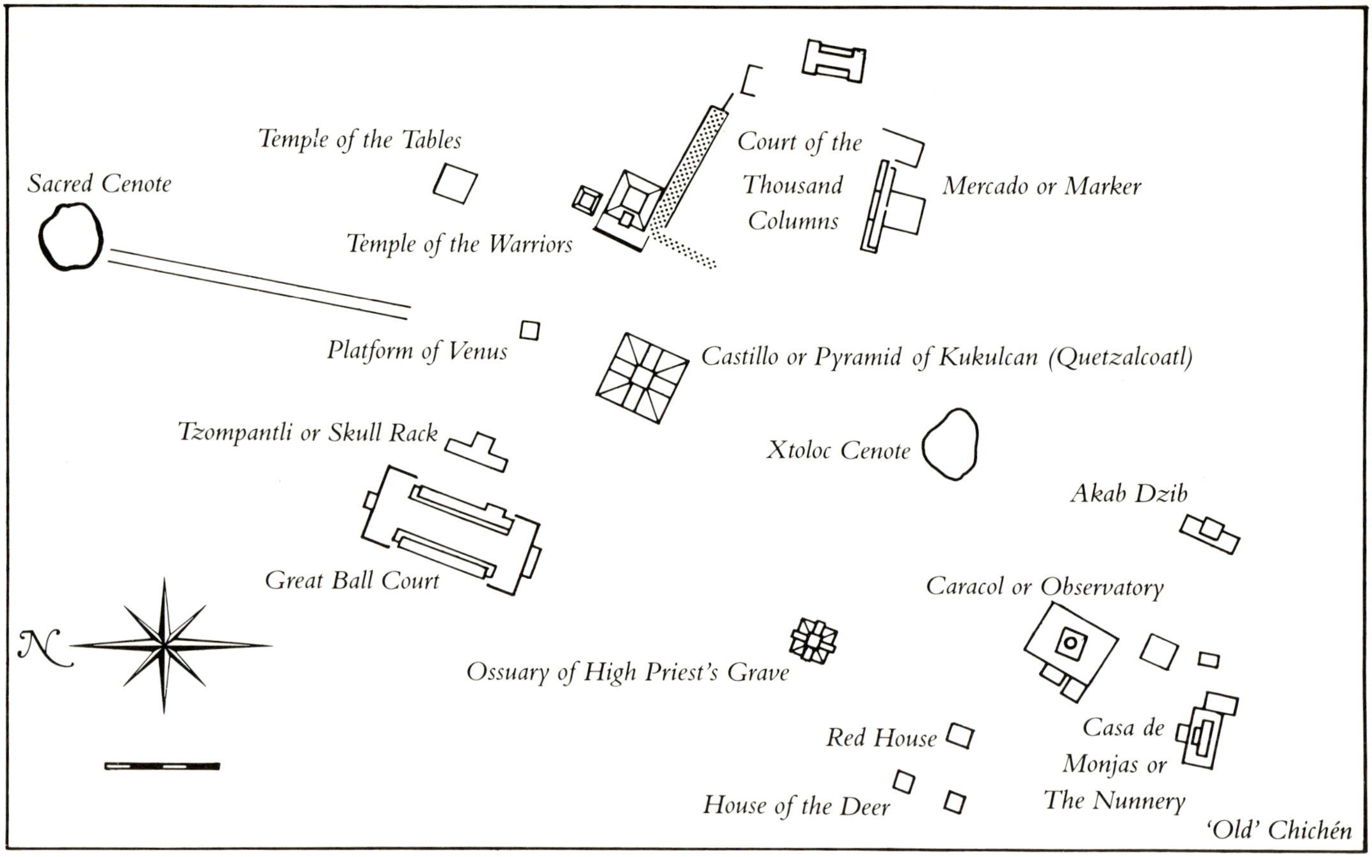

12 *Plan of Chichén Itzá*

Yet another barrier to understanding Chichén Itzá is that in contrast to the extensive genealogical and historical hieroglyphic texts found at earlier Classic Maya cities such as Tikal and Palenque, Chichén Itzá's inscriptions are relatively brief, encompass a very short period in the late ninth and early tenth centuries, and are rarely associated with monuments in the centre of the city. To compound the problem, there were other differences between the northern and southern Maya in dating systems, writing styles and events recorded, making interpretation harder. These difficult texts at Chichén however, are being read and analysed by epigraphers who have determined that they, too, are historical in content (Kowalski 1985; Krochock 1988).

Who was responsible for building and occupying Chichén Itzá, and when, remain unresolved issues. The traditional view was that Chichén Itzá was built by ethnic Maya during the Late Classic. Subsequently, Toltec invaders from Tula invaded and took over the city towards the end of the tenth century (for example Seler 1909; Tozzer 1930 & 1957). According to this theory, the invaders constructed buildings in a hybrid Maya-Toltec style in the heart of the city ('New' Chichén Itzá), leaving intact earlier 'pure' Maya structures nearby ('Old' Chichén Itzá). Now, however, there is a wide range of opinion regarding what actually happened at the site, with some experts (for example Lincoln 1985) rejecting the idea that the Toltecs ever occupied the city, while others (for example Kelley 1984) still support it. Indeed, the art and architecture of Chichén Itzá is of a higher quality and more heterogeneous than that of Tula, the supposed invader, and some of the features previously cited as being typically Toltec at Chichén Itzá are not present at Tula, or are traceable to Maya origins. Furthermore, the distinction between 'Maya' and 'Toltec' warriors proposed by Tozzer (1930) cannot be sustained on close examination of the many figures represented at the site.

Twenty years ago the great British Mayanist J. Eric Thompson (1970) proposed that Chontal-speaking Maya left their homeland along the Gulf Coast in the ninth century to penetrate the southern Maya lowlands and, at a later date, the Yucatán peninsula. These aggressive traders, known as Putun or Itzá, shared many traits with their non-Maya neighbours and introduced a number of new architectural, iconographic and epigraphic features at the sites they occupied, most notably at Seibal, Guatemala and at Chichén Itzá (Kowalski in press).

Recent analyses of hieroglyphic lintels, the reliefs of the Temple of the Warriors, and building types point to a social structure quite different from that of the hierarchical, patrilineal one of the southern Maya sites, hinting at the introduction of new social norms by the Itzá (Krochock 1988; Kristan-Graham n.d.; Lincoln n.d.). Certainly the shift in art from the Late Classic emphasis on the individual ruler to the group, exemplified by the many processions and group scenes evident at the site, reflects an ideological change. Whether or not the Itzá were replaced at Chichén Itzá by the Toltecs is still debated, but the argument for a neat separation between Maya and Toltec periods of occupation, represented by distinct artistic styles, has been considerably weakened.

Adela Breton's work in copying the Upper Temple of the Jaguars murals is particularly significant, and not only because murals in good condition are a rare find in the Maya area. They represent the most complete and graphic depiction of Maya warfare and its aftermath since the Late Classic murals at Bonampak, Chiapas. An unusual feature for Pre-Columbian painting is the inclusion of landscape elements like the red hills that seem to represent a locale far from Chichén Itzá, perhaps even Oaxaca, as one scholar has suggested (A. Miller 1977: 211-213). The two war chiefs, identified by a sun disc in one case and a feathered serpent in the other (Pl.19, upper right) appear not only in the paintings several times, but also on the wooden lintel over the doorway, as the central figures in the carved reliefs of the Lower Temple of the Jaguars, and elsewhere at the site. Whether they are antagonists, allies or father and son is a current scholarly controversy, but there is no doubt that they are key players in the history and politics of Chichén Itzá (A. Miller 1977; Lincoln 1985; Freidel n.d.).

Miss Breton's comments on the iconography of the scenes she copied at Chichén Itzá, while laconic, were astute. Her familiarity with the reliefs and murals of the site led her to conclude that local historical persons and events were represented, a conclusion supported by subsequent scholarship. Noting, for example, that what seems to be a jaguar throne occurs in the south vault of the Upper Temple of the Jaguars murals (Pl.20, lower row, to left of heart sacrifice), she speculated that a similar bench still in place at the entrance to the Lower Temple of the Jaguars was actually used by the 'sun-hero' (Breton 1917: 193). He is shown seated on a jaguar throne elsewhere at the site, including the reliefs of the Lower Temple of the Jaguars (Maudslay 1889-1902, vol.3: pl. 50).

While she did not speculate on the ethnic identity of the participants in the various dramas depicted on the walls of Chichén Itzá, Miss Breton (1906a: 169) did point to the existence of what she called 'different race types', distinguished by height, build, and skin tone.

Noting that the location of the shields painted on the Upper Temple of the Jaguars walls seems to have been fixed first, before the placement of the figures, she (Breton 1906a: 167) thought that their positions might be worthy of study by a mathematician or astronomer. One scholar has recently proposed that the paintings themselves and the events documented are arranged according to the cycles of the sun and the planet Venus, with sun and serpent figures placed in positions that replicate the movement of the two celestial bodies (Coggins 1984: 157 ff). Adela Breton (1906a: 167) also remarked on the 'glow of soft warm colour' of the Upper Temple walls when illuminated by the April and May afternoon sun. Another writer suggests that the structure was deliberately orientated toward the solar zenith sunset in late May, at which time sunlight penetrates the inner temple and illuminates the murals (Milbrath n.d.).

Miss Breton observed that the walls of the outer chamber of the Upper Temple had been painted, but exposure to the elements after the roof caved in had largely destroyed them except for a few shields indicating that more battle scenes were depicted. Inside, she could see traces of an earlier coat in a red and blue 'diaper pattern' (Breton 1906a: 166). She noted that the later murals had been repaired and recoloured after the plaster cracked, and that the Maya had also left graffiti scratched in the plaster. Although a long- established tradition in the study of Western and Asian art, identifying the work of individual artists or schools of art is a relatively new field of endeavour for Mayanists, and has been largely limited to polychrome ceramics and the occasional well-preserved corpus of stone monuments. While copying the murals, however, Adela Breton (1906a: 167) thought she recognised the hands of two artists at work, one of whom worked swiftly, without outline, in dry colour that peels off easily (Pl.19). The second, more methodical painter, outlined his figures in red on the damp plaster and painted his colours in true fresco, with a few details added when the plaster was dry (Fig.10).

Largely buried beneath a modern town, the site of Acancéh has not been subject to the intensive excavation and mapping of Chichén Itzá. Its most visible remains are a large Pre-Classic pyramid on the town plaza and the massive eight-metre high Acropolis, both of which were briefly explored by Mexican and American archaeologists (Fernández 1939; Brainerd 1958; Andrews 1965). Adela Breton's notes indicate that she spent five weeks at the site copying the frieze of the Palace of the Stuccoes (Tozzer 1957: 270).

The function of the small four-chambered structure situated on the Acropolis is unknown: given its dimensions and plan it may have served as a temple. Built around AD 700, it had been covered over at a later date by another structure when northern Maya architectural decoration changed from modelled stucco to cut-stone mosaics. As a result, the brilliant polychrome relief of the upper façade was fortuitously preserved in a region where intact stucco exterior ornamentation is rare indeed. It is unfortunate that protective measures were not taken at the time the frieze was discovered, for although a tin roof was installed over the façade in 1940, of the twenty-one figures, remains of only four are relatively complete now, and the colour has long since disappeared.

Although Miss Breton states that she traced the façade, it is difficult to imagine how she might have done so over the fragile high relief of the stucco frieze. In any case, in her typically thorough fashion, she completed one set of pen and ink drawings and another in watercolour, both done to scale on sheets of paper accommodating four to six figures each. The large raptorial birds that framed each end of the frieze as well as its narrow upper and lower borders were copied on separate sheets of paper.

Adela Breton (1908) reported the discovery of the Palace, but never published her watercolours. The best-known drawing of the frieze made by W. von den Steinen, prepared for an article on the frieze by Eduard Seler (Seler 1902–23), provided the basis for subsequent copies of the frieze. William Gates was preparing to publish a coloured version of the façade shortly before his death in 1940 (Gates collection, Harold B. Lee Library, Brigham Young University, Provo, Utah). The most accurate and reliable drawing is that of Adela Breton, the first artist at the site.

13 (left) Watercolour of the remains of mural 13 from a building at Acancéh, showing a standing male figure wearing a brilliant blue feather headdress. Ea 8184c

14 (right) Watercolour of the remains of a mural from the 'small chamber' at Acancéh. This and Fig. 13 show how little was left of th murals in 1907. The building and paintings are now completely lost. Ea 8184b

In addition to copying the façade of the Palace of the Stuccoes, Miss Breton also reproduced some now-lost mural paintings whose exact location is unclear, but which appear to have been in the structure directly north of the Palace, probably built slightly afterwards. Although Seler (1915a: 403- 404) illustrates and discusses a few hieroglyphs from wallpaintings, the existence of human figures was not mentioned until Adela Breton's copies of the paintings surfaced recently at Bristol. The hieroglyphs and figures are very fragmentary but both appear to be Late Classic in style (Figs. 13,14). The remains of a Maya Long Count date are present in one mural, probably commemorating an historical event, while a hieroglyphic phrase may document ritual blood-letting. In one scene reproduced here (Fig.13), all that remains of a standing male figure are his legs and the sweeping, brilliant blue feathers of his headdress and costume, reminiscent of the Bonampak murals.

The stucco relief was not only a remarkable find for its state of preservation, but because its composition and subject matter are unique in the Maya area. The Acancéh frieze depicts a procession of framed figures facing in the same direction, rather than the more typical hierarchical arrangement of deity masks or ruler portraits centred over the doorways. The twenty-one figures are divided into two rows, the upper including essentially celestial beings, like birds and an anthropomorphised bat, and the lower representing terrestrial creatures such as serpents, frogs, and a howler monkey (Pl.25). The sole human occurs in the top row. Animals, while common in minor arts like jade carving and painted ceramics, are rarely featured in Maya monumental art. The processional arrangement of framed anthropomorphic animals recalls the murals of Teotihuacán rather than Maya façades or wallpainting.

Although Teotihuacán was in decline by the time the Palace was built, echoes of the great Early Classic central Mexican metropolis continued to be felt in the art and architecture of the Maya area after its demise. Among other features that recall Teotihuacán are the figures' speech scrolls, their headdresses and jewellery, the decorative waterband above the frieze (Pl.26), and the vessels (seen in X-ray view) just below it (Pl.25). But none of these elements is duplicated at Teotihuacán itself, and the naturalistic proportions of the figures and their animated gestures are typically Maya. The modelled stucco medium, too, is alien to Teotihuacán.

The eclectic style of the stucco frieze is directly comparable with the recently-discovered murals of Cacaxtla, near Puebla, and the sculptural reliefs of Xochicalco, Morelos, also published by Breton (1906b). Both display strong Maya influence and may even have been created by Maya artists. Like the sculptor of the Palace of the Stuccoes, however, these artists did not simply copy the art of the distant culture, but combined stylistic and iconographic elements from various sources in original and unexpected ways. The political events that led to these new artistic expressions are still not well understood, but the time period in which all three sites flourished was characterised by an unusually vigorous exchange of goods and ideas throughout Meso-America.

Adela Breton must have been aware of her pivotal role in copying the vanishing art of Chichén Itzá and Acancéh. But she could not have predicted that eighty years later both sites would still be at the centre of a lively scholarly debate, with the corpus of works she preserved considered one of the major keys to resolving a myriad of issues. Although of different eras, both sites demonstrate the Maya facility for skilfully absorbing and adapting foreign influence. Our view of Chichén Itzá's history has been radically altered in recent years, becoming more complex rather than simpler. But instead of treating it as a conquered Maya city upon which an alien art style was imposed, it may be more appropriate to view Chichén Itzá as a late Maya Rome, adopting the art and architecture of its subjects, trading partners, and predecessors, and perhaps even accepting works or the artists themselves as booty (Schele and Miller 1986: 142, 218-220).

In the case of Acancéh, the lack of extensive excavation at the site has made it particularly difficult to evaluate its cultural connections within and outside the Maya area. As a result, Miss Breton's copy of the unique façade of the Palace of the Stuccoes is especially valuable. Typically during the Late Classic, minor central Mexican motifs may be grafted onto essentially Maya forms, as in the use of Teotihuacán elements in the costume of Maya rulers. The Acancéh frieze, however, represents real syncretism in which Maya and central Mexican sculptural techniques, styles, and iconography are woven smoothly together to create an entirely new form.

Adela Breton understood that the preservation of deteriorating works of art would not only benefit future scholarship, but could also provide unexpected aesthetic pleasure for viewers accustomed to seeing Pre-Columbian monuments as they generally appear today: a monochrome, neutral hue. She wanted others to experience what the Maya had seen when their buildings were new, remarking once that 'these people *saw* in colour and light and shade' (Breton 1906a: 167). Fortunately for us, so did Adela Breton.

Dr Virginia E. Miller

'If I could have Pablo & the horses ...'

For at least some of her travels in Mexico, Adela Breton was 'accompanied only by one Indian, who was devoted to her' (Fallaize, 1923). Most of what is known about Pablo Solorio comes from the few letters extant from the indefatigable pen of Adela Breton. Pablo was employed as her servant, but seems to have been a friend as well, or treated as a young relative, and the letters often spoke of how dependent she was on him:

> I shall be like a violinist who has lost the one instrument he can play on.
> [AB to Tozzer (Don Alfredo), 20 Sept 1904 PM]

Much of Adela Breton's travelling was on horseback, and Pablo looked after the horses, el Chico and el Moro (Fig.15): he also looked after her house at Chichén Itzá and did the buying and cooking of food.

Adela Breton frequently wrote of the hardships of life in Mexico, and Pablo presumably shared them with her:

> ... the difficulty in going far into Mexico is the impossibility of getting any food ... I used to live chiefly on air & a few pea-nuts for the long riding journeys, - 30 miles without any breakfast, & then some frijol broth
> [AB to Bowditch, 1st August 1916 PM]

And yet she loved an outdoor life, and bemoaned the many illnesses which kept her confined to bed or house. Soon after Pablo's death, she wrote that:

> If I could have Pablo & the horses, an outdoor life & tortillas I should soon be better ...
> [AB to Tozzer (Don Alfredo), 18 May 1906 PM]

and years later she was still writing, with regard to her health:

> I wish some one would give me some out-door work. How often I have longed for Pablo & my horses (Fig.16).
> [AB to Tozzer (Don Alfredo), 15 September 1919 PM]

Adela Breton seems to have admired Pablo Solorio, though not everyone shared this view of him. Edward Thompson, United States consul to the Yucatan, owner of the Chichén Itzá site and amateur archaeologist, thought Pablo prying and meddling, and his wife

> '... has taken a violent dislike to poor P.'
> [AB to Tozzer, 8 May 1904]

Adela Breton, however, praised his character highly:

15 Photograph of Pablo Solorio with the horses el Moro and el Chico. Ea 8444

16 Photograph of Pablo Solorio with the horses at the Ibarra ferry, near Guadalajara. Ea 8444

> ...he had such beautiful thoughts, & such a wonderful mind altogether, tho' he was reserved with strangers, he talked to me as if he had been Dante or Shakespeare.
> [AB to Tozzer (Don Alfredo), 20 September 1904 PM]

Mrs Thompson's dislike of Pablo was enough to make Adela Breton think of not returning to work at Chichén Itzá until the Thompsons sold up.

> Pablo usually gets on admirably with the varied characters one meets in travelling, so I know it is not his fault.
> [AB to Tozzer, 8 May 1904 PM]

Pablo Solorio came from the village of Churumuco, in Michoacan state. His age and other personal details are not known, nor how he came to work for Miss Breton. He had a wife, but no mention is made in the letters of children. Of one stay at Chichén Itzá, copying the mural and caryatids in the Upper Temple of the Jaguars , Adela Breton wrote:

> I could have stayed 6 months longer with pleasure, but Pablo's wife wants him back
> [AB to Tozzer, 9 May 1903]

He was well educated, presumably in Spanish:

> Pablo writes that he is very well & perfectly happy! so that is something in this sad world (Fig.17).
> [AB to Tozzer, 4 September 1903 PM]

Adela Breton suggested to Professor Putnam of the Peabody Museum that Pablo could collect antiquities for the museum;

> ... he is a trustworthy observer & could make notes of how the things are found in connection with bodies
> [AB to Putnam, 19 June 1904 HUA]

Pablo collected antiquities, which he gave to Adela Breton.

> My servant Pablo Solorio brought me such a nice little collection of antiquities this time from the neighbourhood of his village ... Almost anywhere, a little digging produces objects of shell, jadeite, good lances of chert & obsidian, jars & quantities of beads & ornaments
> [AB to Putnam, 19 June 1904 HUA]

Much of the collection was on loan to the Museum at Bristol, and after his death Adela Breton wrote to the Superintendent, Mr Quick, asking that Pablo Solorio be acknowledged as the collector.

He appears in many of Adela Breton's paintings and photographs, a small figure sitting beside a ruin or a smiling figure on horseback. He also tried his hand at drawing and painting: he borrowed her sketchbook and paints or used the back of one of her drawings, but he was not an artist (Fig.18).

At Chichén Itzá, she relied greatly on Pablo for several seasons. She lived during some visits in a wooden hut in the grounds of the Thompson's hacienda, and Pablo kept house for her (Fig.19). Whilst she was away, Thompson obviously took it over, as she complained.

> It is not quite fair of Mr. Thompson to use my house, considering what a tumble-down dirty shed it was before Pablo took it in hand...
> [AB to Tozzer, 18 November 1903 PM]

17 (left) Photograph of the interior of Adela Breton's house at Chichén Itzá, 'Pablo reading a letter'. Ea 11101c
18 (right) Watercolour of the Ball Court at Chichén Itzá by Pablo Solorio, painted in a sketchbook. Ea 9496

19 (above) Photograph showing the interior of Adela Breton's house at Chichén Itzá, showing Pablo Solorio standing by the table. Ea 11101d
20 (below) Photograph of Pablo Solorio beside Miss Breton's tent, at Atlixtaca, Guerrero State, February 1898. Ea 8453

On her next visit she had to camp in the Upper Temple of the Jaguars, but where Pablo slept is not known.
Life at Chichén Itzá was not easy; years later Adela Breton was to recall:

> Food, fever, & suffering from bites of many kinds ... The devotion of poor good Pablo, & his almost daily walks to Pisté to bring tortillas, platanos, eggs, enabled me to survive.
> [AB to Tozzer, 22 August 1921 PM]

It was ironic that Adela Breton, who was in delicate health all her life, endured all the rigours of Mexican life (Fig.20), and yet Pablo Solorio, born and bred to it, died of fever:

> ... a victim to the hardships of camping in Yucatan ...
> [AB to Quick. 30 January 1905 BCM]

> He had no strength to resist an illness. His poor wife.
> [AB to Tozzer (Don Alfredo), 20 September 1904 PM]

> If nothing can be heard of Pablo, I shall almost feel I ought to go myself & try to find out, - only it would be carrying out a dreadfully prophetic dream I had two years ago, & unluckily did not heed sufficiently.
> [AB to Tozzer (Don Alfredo), 14 November 1904 PM]

> I cannot tell you how *dreadful* this uncertainty is to me about poor Pablo. I know now what so many English homes have suffered in our many wars, when some gallant son has been reported "missing" & never heard of again.
> [AB to Tozzer (Don Alfredo), 23 November 1904 PM]

Adela Breton felt guilt over his death - he was in the Yucatán because of her and he suffered because of her:

> I was very disinclined to leave him all those days in Merida ... Now I grieve that I did not go round by Mexico & see him safe on his way.
> [AB to Tozzer, 20 September 1904 PM]

> I have had much remorse for sacrificing him. One scarcely knew what one was doing in that struggle to exist & work.
> [AB to Tozzer, 22 August 1921 PM]

It seems to have taken several months for Adela Breton to find out, through letters and friends, what had happened to Pablo:

> I have had an extremely sad & painful time. My worst fears were realized, as poor Pablo died of yellow fever at the Hospital at Vera Cruz, & *everything* combined to make a most terribly tragic ending to the years of happy travel which I owed him.
> [AB to Mead, 30 March 1905 HUA]

Sue Giles

The Caryatid figures from the Temple of the Jaguars

The following, translated from Spanish, is Adela Breton's own account of the discovery and rediscovery of the stone figures from the Upper Temple of the Jaguars, Chichén Itzá.

What is most surprising about the well-known ruins of Chichén Itzá is the abundance of realistic sculpture: apart from the more or less symbolic gigantic heads, snakes and fret decorations that are on the outside of the buildings, inside them are many reliefs depicting warriors, sometimes life-size, all painted in colours...

The Upper Temple of the Tigers, 'Temple A', has been described by Mr A Maudslay, Dr W. H. Holmes and Dr A. Le Plongeon in their books. Its façade faces the *Tlachtli* (Fig.21), towering to a height of over eight metres. A staircase with five steps leads to the entrance of the first room, between two pillars representing gigantic feathered serpents with their heads on the floor, facing outwards, their bodies raised, and their rattles forming the capitals.

The upper part of the façade and the ceiling in this first room collapsed many years ago, leaving a pile of worked stones and soil which made it difficult for Stephens and Catherwood (in 1841) to get through the door to the second room. The pictures of battles on the walls have disappeared almost completely, but with difficulty one can make out some circular shields from which it is deduced that the paintings were similar to the beautiful old scenes depicted in the inner room.

Dr and Mrs Le Plongeon in 1882 cleared the outside room, throwing all the fallen stones over the wall, and then, between the serpent columns and the door of the inner room, appeared an altar of stone supported by fifteen statues. (In 'Queen Moo', the book published by Dr Le Plongeon, there is a photograph of the altar as it appeared when they cleared the rubble.) The statues, 775 mm high, were arranged in three rows of five. Their arms were raised and their feet apart as if to better support the heavy weight of the slabs they were holding. In the photograph one can see a part of the slabs, but the force of the vault's collapse had broken them into pieces that were mixed up with all the other debris.

After photographing and numbering the statues, Dr Le Plongeon buried them, so nobody knew where they were.When I came to Chichén in 1900 I saw a piece of engraved stone and asked Mr Maudsley and Mr E. Thompson, owner of the property in Chichén, of what it was part. They did not know about the existence of the altar, but, helped by the picture published in 'Queen Moo' I looked around and little by little gathered enough pieces to reconstruct the altar table in part. The other pieces were probably in the pile of rubble at the foot of the wall, if only I could have found a labourer to do the work, which is something I have not been able to get in six attempts.

21 (opposite) Plan of Ball Court at Chichén Itzá, after Maudslay.

From the remains of the slabs that I found it can be deduced that there were four slabs together, each 1 metre square and 155 mm thick. On them was sculptured in low relief one figure standing and another one about to kneel down, with his atlatl in his right hand, offering another weapon with his left to the standing character. A feathered serpent slithers between the two. Around the edges of the slabs there were very finely engraved reliefs representing, in miniature, seated chiefs with their ranks in hieroglyphics.

Once the table of the altar had been found, we had to look for the statues. I talked about them with the late Don Santiago Bolio, Inspector of the ruins, and he noticed observantly that one of the stones in the floor seemed to be loose. He started digging with his labourers and there they found the fifteen statues, in good condition, having been very carefully buried by Dr Le P. Their cloaks of long feathers and their other decorations still had remainders of the colours that at one time made this building shine.

This happened in 1902 and Don S. B. informed the Ministry of our discovery. In March 1903 he received orders to send the statues to Mexico City and he came to Chichen with some labourers. They lowered the statues, tied up with ropes, down the wall, causing

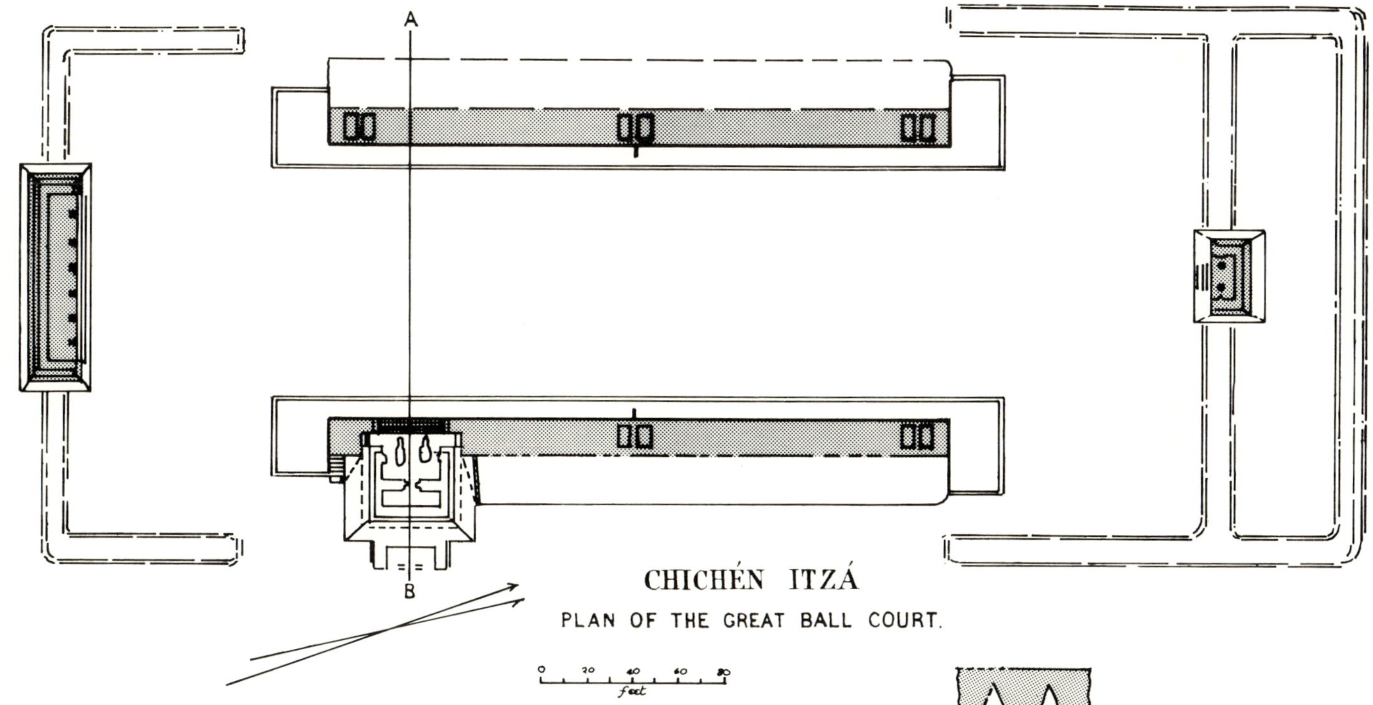

CHICHÉN ITZÁ

PLAN OF THE GREAT BALL COURT.

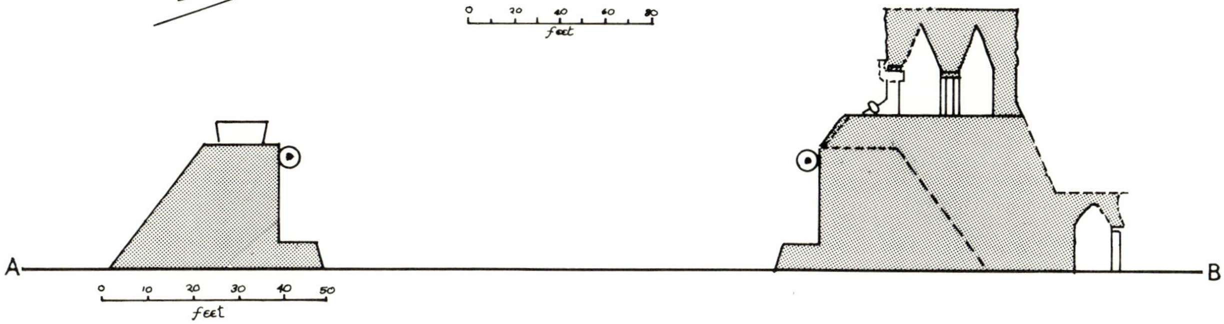

SECTION THROUGH THE LINE A.B.

> quite a lot of damage with the inevitable knocks against the stone wall. Fortunately when they were half way down Mr E. Thompson arrived with a winch and thanks to this the others were taken down without difficulty. They took them in carts to Citas where they were packed and so they arrived in Mexico City. After lying forgotten in the Customs, they at last arrived at the National Museum in 1908.
>
> It is necessary to study these statues in depth to be able to understand their meaning fully, and above all it is essential to study them in the way they were arranged. Before they were taken away, when they were still in Chichén, I placed them in rows (Pl.15) helped by the numbers written on each one by Dr Le P and I took some photographs (I also made - very much in a hurry because suddenly Sr Bolio came to take them away - drawings of each one, seen from the front and the back) realizing then that the first row on the south side, the ones numbered II, III and IV, seem to belong to the same family. They wear the same type of cloak, of yellow feathers scattered with green ones, their headdresses are very similar, and their faces have the same shape.
> [AB manuscript n.d., HF 7705 BCM]

There were similar altars in two other temples at Chichén Itzá, the Temple of the Tables and the Temple of the Warriors (Pl.17). Both of these altars are still in position, one collapsed and one standing. Dr Le Plongeon presumably buried the Upper Temple of the Jaguars altar supports for safe keeping.

It was almost by chance that Adela Breton was still at Chichén Itzá in 1903 when Inspector Bolio arrived to remove the statues. She and the Thompsons were engaged in a battle of wills:

> It was rather amusing, and very annoying, to stay on by main force as it were, against their will. But my work became more important as I went on, & I could not be driven away.
> [AB to Tozzer, 9 May 1903 PM]

Adela Breton was concentrating on the mural painting in the Temple, working on the south west wall, and interrupted this work to make her drawings of the Caryatids.

> Then the Inspector suddenly appeared with 2 carts, to carry off the statues, & knowing how they would be knocked about, I had to make drawings of them, which took a fortnight of hard work.
> [AB to Tozzer, 9 May 1903 PM]

They were taken away two at a time, so she had time to draw them all (Pls.8-14). Adela Breton writes of 'drawings' although the watercolour paintings in the collection are hardly that. She may have worked up her rough drawings later, but there are only a few roughs, not one for each caryatid, and as Miss Breton seems rarely to have thrown anything away, it is likely that these finished watercolours are her sketches, made 'very much in a hurry'. The smaller copies may have been done later, from the originals.

Adela Breton, following Le Plongeon, called the statues caryatids, and was convinced that this was the correct name for them. To her, they were women; Dr Seler thought they were men and thus Atlanteans; Le Plongeon thought some were women. Miss Breton listed several reasons in support of her belief:

1 It is improbable that there would be "some women" among men ... Mexican Indian women always keep quite apart from the men in public functions.
2 They are very much shorter in proportion than the *16* warriors ...
3 The *profile view* of the face & neck is very different to that of the warriors, much softer...

They have no weapons ... and they all have more or less garments, whereas the 16 warriors (on the door jambs) only have the girdle.
[AB to Mead, 6 November 1905 HUA]

A stronger reason though, was gut reaction.

One needs to study the statues carefully as I did when drawing them, & as I lived with them for two months, I felt they were women. They did not approve of me at first - not understanding the modern woman!
[AB to Mead, 6 November 1905 HUA]

Adela Breton was, at the time of writing, 55 years old!
She looked at the caryatids from a different point of view to other observers.

You have no idea how beautiful they are, if one brings oneself down to their level.I had to sit on the ground to do them.
[AB to Tozzer, 9 May 1903 PM]

As Adela Breton wrote in her account, the statues 'still had remainders of the colours' on them; in her paintings of them she filled out those remainders, leaving blank only those areas which gave no clue to their original colours (Pl.14).
The caryatids are still in the National Museum of Anthropology in Mexico City (Pl.16). Four are on display (as of 1989).

Adela C Breton and Sue Giles

Some Mexican Portrait Clay Figures

(Reprinted from MAN, 3, 1903. Published by the Royal Anthropological Institute of Great Britain and Ireland.)

The portrait figures from which these drawings were made came from a mound or tumulus near Etzatlan, in the State of Jalisco, Mexico.

The town of Etzatlan is about 70 miles north-west of Guadalajara, and at the first coming of the Spaniards was the capital of a state or canton forming one of a confederation of states called Chimalhuacan, inhabited by peaceful and civilised communities speaking the Nahuatl language.

The mound in question is three leagues north of the modern town, on a level field belonging to the hacienda of Guadalupe, and the owner caused it to be excavated early in 1896(Fig.24). Unfortunately there was no skilled supervision, no data were secured, and most of the figures were broken.

Two oblong elevations near the mound, now only a few feet high, may have been sites of former buildings. The mound itself was rounded and about 40 feet high.A wide trench was dug from both the north and the south sides towards its centre and almost through, and about half the mound had been cleared away to the ground level. Nearly in the middle, on the south side, the workmen came, at a few feet below the outer level, to a layer of charcoal and soft, loose, brown earth, in which they found a skeleton resting on a whitey-grey compound, a sort of grey clay. The skull was finely developed. Above this they found the figures.

The mound was composed of a core of very hard earth (there were stones which looked as it they had been used to pound or flatten down the earth), upon that were several feet of mixed stones and earth, the stones unhewn and varying in size up to two feet square, and then more earth covering the whole.

I made sketches of some of the figures and was able to bring away two, which are now in the Bristol Museum (Fig.22). Some remained at the hacienda, and others were given to the owner's friends. There were at least 20; two of them were not shown. Señor D Mauro Villaseñor, a judge a the neighbouring town of Ahualulco, had two, a man and a woman, some shell bracelets, jade amulets and beads, and cut shell and stone ornaments. He also had a cylinder of extremely hard polished stone which he thought was the stem of a pipe, and some very small flat bits of white metal - not silver - with holes.

It appears to have been the custom in that part of Mexico to place portrait-figures round a tumulus, probably representing members of the deceased's household. A herbalist who, in the course of wanderings in a deserted part of eastern Jalisco, had come across several burial places, told me he had found this the case. Near Chapala two female figures were found together, one apparently the chief lady, dignified and

22 (opposite) Photograph of the finds from the Mound of Guadalupe given to Miss Breton, see Cat.Nos.149-158

smiling, carrying her platter of offerings on her left shoulder. The other, of lower birth, had a painful expression of horror in her face and clutched her hair with one hand while the other was outstretched in seeming effort to ward off some terrible fate.

Those of Guadalupe seem all prosperous and happy. The head lady (Pl.32) bears her offering to the gods and wears armlets like those found in the mound. Her face and body are painted or tattooed, and she appears to have a ceremonial symbolic garment with a pattern of grecques. She has several rings in each ear and a nose ornament. The same type of face and figure may still be met in the Indian villages, and it represents a matron of the highest qualities - capable, hard working, kindly, an admirable housewife, and the best mother in the world. Two other female figures may have been her handmaids (Pl.33). They are all of coarse clay, from a quarter to one third of an inch thick, one 12 inches high, and the others 18 and 20 inches. Two men were painted with great detail; one of them (Pl.34) was admirable as a work of art, showing great mastery both of modelling and colour.

One of the three armlets which I have is a plain flat band of shell. Of the other two figured one has 26 frogs carved in low relief (a small piece is broken off), and the other has four two-headed snakes and four frogs alternately (Fig.23). Small shell frogs and beads of various shapes may have been parts of necklaces, and there are some curious small shell silhouette figures. All these are in the Bristol Museum. They are specimens from a great quantity at the hacienda.

Frogs seem to have represented some Mexican divinity, as at Guanaxuato there are some rocks above the city which have the appearance of frogs, and were regarded as tutelar gods by the Indians. Offerings were made and dances performed there. A carved frog stands by one of the rock-baths on the hill of Texcozingo, near Texcoco, where Netzahualcoyotl had his famous gardens, and I possessed a celt of dark stone, shaped into a frog and polished, from Zacatlan, on the border of the States of Hidalgo and Puebla.

As this mound is near the great obsidian workings of Teuchitlan, where miles of hillside are strewn with refuse cuttings, one would expect to find good implements in it, but I am not aware this was so. Two triangular flakes of unusual shape and some 'cores' were all that I saw. There was a manufactory of these prismatic objects, usually called cores, on the hill, now an island, in the Lake of Maddalena, close to Etzatlan. Dozens of rejects may be picked up there, whereas among the myriads of flakes of all sizes and shapes at Teuchitlan there are none.

Adela. C. Breton

23 (above) Pen and ink drawing of the shell jewellery from the Mound of Guadalupe, see Cat.Nos.152-155

24 (right) Pen and ink sketch of the excavation of the Mound of Guadalupe, May 1895. From photograph. Ea 8444

The Wall Paintings at Chichen Itza

(Reprinted from Proceedings, 15th International Congress of Americanists, Quebec, 1906)

Students of Central American archaeology have scarcely as yet appreciated the important part that painting formerly played in the decorative art of that region. The first explorers were overwhelmed by the grandeur and strangeness of the ruins, and were too fully occupied in making plans of the structure, and moulds of the reliefs and monoliths, to have time for more than hasty notes of the colours on them. This was unfortunate, for where the buildings were covered with debris, when first excavated, the colours were often fresh, and exposure to the weather has since destroyed them.

From the remains still visible, it is evident that all the sculptured parts were coloured and that the colours were more or less symbolic. Those people *saw* in colour and light and shade. That is why mere outline copies of the sculptures, and casts set up in a light for which they were not intended, give a very inadequate idea of the actual effect. The colour is also a great help towards understanding the subjects.

At Chichen Itza there was a remarkable development of Art; not only were the columns, door posts and interior walls of some of the buildings covered with coloured reliefs representing personages and events, but many chambers were entirely painted in fresco with historical scenes.

These wall paintings are of the highest interest, not only from the point of view of archaeology but from that of Art. In colour, drawing and design they can hold their own anywhere, although to modern eyes they may appear quaint and childlike as do those of the Early Italian school. As they are, unfortunately, much destroyed, they cannot be seen fairly in a hurried visit, but after studying them day by day, and when the light is good, one comes to feel a great admiration for artists who could so skilfully transfer the bright harmonious tints of their sunset skies to an intractable material like plaster.

Mr Thompson, Dr Le Plongeon and Mr Maudslay copied some portions of these paintings, but from various reasons their copies have not become known as they deserved, and it was at Mr Maudslay's suggestion that I attempted the great task of copying the whole series...

In Temple A (or Temple of the Tigers) [Upper Temple of the Jaguars] the walls of the outer chamber were painted, but owing to the roof having fallen in, they were exposed to the weather and only a few round shields are now left, showing that the subjects were battles as in the inner chamber. This latter has suffered from the local tourist who has written names all over it, and also from copyists who have outlined the figures in pencil, or worse still, with a red line which at first sight appears original until one sees that it crosses gaps in the plaster. Still, with care and patience something can be saved from the wreck which becomes each year more deplorable, now that the removal of the trees and plants which protected the exterior allows the tropic rains to pour down the walls.

The Paintings were not the first decoration of the building. Traces of a previous coat can be seen here and there, showing a kind of diaper pattern in red and blue. But they were done a sufficiently long time before the place was abandoned for a crack in the plaster to have required mending and recolouring. There are also *graffiti* scratched in the plaster by ancient devotees.

METHOD. - There were certainly two artists employed, and their methods were different. One was a master who knew exactly what he meant to do, and did it in a calm methodical way, with certainty and swiftness of brush in the sweeping outlines. The other, more impetuous, dashed in figures just as they came into his head, after he had fixed the positions of the shields. These positions (at any rate on the south and south-west walls), are not hap-hazard, and it might be worth while for a mathematician or astronomer to study them. This artist understood how to place one tint over another to give a rich and glowing effect. He put in few outlines, and the greater part of his work is in dry colour which comes off easily, or peels away in patches. I attribute to him about half the work, - the north and south walls, and the middle and north end of the east wall.

The other artist drew all his figures carefully in red outline on the damp plaster, and also, in true fresco fashion put on his chief masses of colour, while the plaster was damp. This helps to give the delightful varied effect of the tints, only enough colour being mixed for each day's work. Then the details were added in dry colours. Few of these are left, and the devices of the shields have been almost entirely obliterated by modern visitors, to insert their own names.

COLOURS USED. - Two reds, two blues, four greens, yellow, white, black, and a purplish tint, and various tones of flesh colour, were used, and although there is no attempt at shading, they are so skilfully contrasted that there is a strong effect of relief. One figure will be light against the ground and another dark. It is only when copying them that one can appreciate the art with which each colour is added to enhance the brilliance and harmony of the whole, as one does in copying Turner's best water colours. It will be understood that these copies give but a poor idea of the glow of soft warm colour when the sun shines in through the narrow door on an afternoon in April or May. Very many of the figures are now mere vague patches of colour, and I have not tried to re-draw them or to do more than reproduce the present fragmentary appearance of the original.

DESCRIPTION.- The long walls of the east and west sides are each divided into three panels. On the west, there is one over the door and those on either side. We suppose that the series begins with the south-west panel, the first to the right on entering...

The south wall is particularly interesting as it shows the methods of attacking lofty places. There are three scaffold-towers on which are warriors, whilst others are climbing a ladder made by notching a long tree-trunk. The personages floating in the air above the houses at the top of this panel will be observed. Part of the painting in the vault is left at this end, with the scene of a sacrifice, and some lean prisoners at one corner. Especially noteworthy are the high, narrow, white banners, like Tibetan prayer-flags, near the bottom of this wall.

The east wall has in its centre panel two life-size personages, one the same as the central figure on the sculptured wall of Chamber E. (the lower Temple of the Tigers)[Lower Temple of the Jaguars], the other perhaps the hero laid out at the bottom of this panel, and also in the panel above the Lintel, and in the border of the North Building of the Ball-Court. The great feathered serpent appears to be in reversed position with his head downwards, judging from the feathers. In the southern panel of this wall, which is very much destroyed, there are several animals and birds amongst the trees at the sides of the fortified village. The northern panel has a series of hills with attacking and defending forces. Here the artist evidently gave a variety of trees and rocks in the landscape, but scarcely anything remains.

On the north wall there is a sun-disk in the centre at the top, and a number of perhaps mythical personages who look as if they had come out of some illuminated manuscript, with their curious red backgrounds and flourishes. The green ground rises diagonally from the bottom to the top. The colours of the figures and the sky are peculiarly rich.

The north end of the west wall has an attack by blue-bodied warriors on a village defended by a fortification coloured red like that of the south east panel. This red object was at first called a canoe until Mr. Maudslay showed that all the houses were inside it, and then it was found that similar representations of defences were to be seen on the so-called slate "palettes" of ancient Egypt.

The border or dado round the lower part of the walls is somewhat similar to those of chamber E. and the North Building. It has personages whom one may perhaps call mythological, entwined with flowery "speeches." The small personage in both borders of the west wall is the same who occurs as a sort of Punchinello in many reliefs as at Palenque and Quirigue.

DIFFERENT RACE-TYPES. - There is a great variety of types. Some of the warriors are very tall and athletic, especially those descending on the South wall, with red feather headdresses. Others are short and plump as in the south west panel. Some profiles have been preserved, though as a rule the shield is so held as to almost cover the face, and where it is visible, the eye has usually been destroyed. There are two good profiles on the Red Hills and some in the South east panel, and the two lama-like persons on a roof in the corner of the south west panel. The flesh-tints vary from the pale yellow of the sun-disk personages and the women, to the dark brown of the defenders of the Red Hills, and of the chiefs sitting before their hut-doors in the bottom row of the south wall.

The speeches have yet to be interpreted, though one may suppose that the warriors cry "Victory or Death" when their speeches are a flourish of red and blue. A man at the top of the south west panel whose atlatl is held downwards as a sign of defeat, has a dejected-looking speech, somewhat like that of a man with bound arms in a Mont Alban relief (Plate XVIII, Batres)...

Adela C. Breton

'An incomparable record ...' Miss Breton and The Museum at Bristol

During her travels in Mexico, Miss Breton acquired a large collection of antiquities, mostly small objects of pottery, stone and shell, many of them collected by her servant, Pablo Solorio. Her own collecting passion was for obsidian, and she brought boxes of this volcanic glass back to her house in Bath.

In 1899 she was preparing to set off again to Mexico, and wished to do something about the collection. The Museum of the Bath Royal Literary and Scientific Institution in Queen Square, Bath was the obvious place: however,

> I have a small case in the Bath Museum but they have no room for more
> [AB to Barker or Bolton, 17 October 1899 BCM]

Her next approach was to Professor C. Lloyd Morgan, a friend and fellow member of the British Association. Lloyd Morgan was a geologist, and lecturer at Bristol's University College. Because of his previous work with and help to the Museum, he had been asked to join the newly formed Advisory Committee of the Museum. Thus he knew W. R. Barker, then Chairman of the Museum Committee, and Miss Breton thought that Bristol would be a good place.

> I am looking about for a Museum in which to deposit my collection of Mexican antiquities ... Do you think Bristol would care for it? ... As it takes up the whole of my dining room (including a long dinner-party table) I am beginning to think it would look better in nice glass cases
> [AB to Lloyd Morgan, 27 August 1899 BCM]

Lloyd Morgan obviously spoke to Barker about it, and later had to prompt him:

> May I remind you of the Mexican collection of which I spoke to you? ... If you care to do anything about it would you write to Miss Breton at Bath ...
> [Lloyd Morgan to Barker, 15 October 1899 BCM]

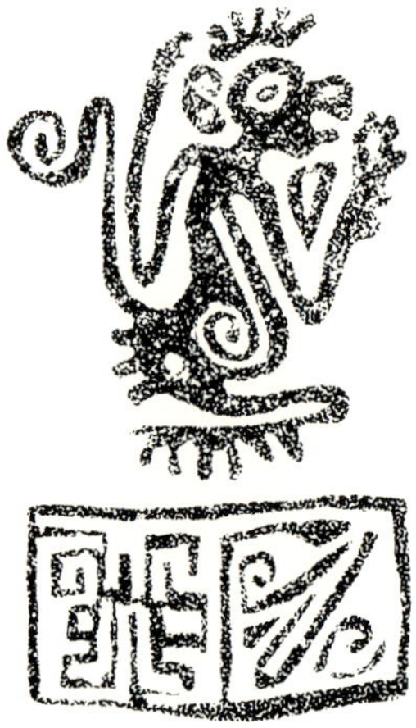

Barker had either misunderstood or forgotten the original conversation, for he assumed that Miss Breton was acting for a brother or father, not that she could be the owner and collector.

> He [Lloyd Morgan] now advises me to write to you respecting a letter he had recd from Mr Breton as to depositing a collection of Mexican antiquities in the Bristol Museum. I presume that Mr Breton is still away from Bath and that Mr Morgan thinks it desirable there should be no further delay ... On behalf of the B. Mus. Com. I beg to assure you that such an addition to our collections wd be very highly valued ...we...

sincerely hope that it may be possible for them to find a place of deposit in our Museum.
[Barker to AB, 16 October 1899 BCM]

Miss Breton was probably used to people making such assumptions: she did not appear to take offence.

For several years I have been travelling in Mexico, visiting the less-known ancient sites, & various places where obsidian was worked, & collecting on the spot, so that all my things have a definite provenance.
[AB to Barker, 17 October 1899 BCM]

A selection of antiquities was made, and put into a glass case at Bristol. Miss Breton did the arrangement and from time to time added to it or changed it.

I had to put the large figures as they are, because the back view is so inelegant ... I should like to add plans, photos, & a small map of the country so as to make the collection really instructive.
[AB to Bolton, 11 January ?1900 BCM]

A suitable case was provided for the large and interesting collection of Mexican objects deposited by Miss Breton of Bath, who has resumed her travels in Mexico.
[Annual Report 1900-1 BCM]

In 1904 a second case was added.

My Mexican cases in the Bristol Art Gallery are doing good in interesting people. A man who has an estate in British Honduras has sent some very good chipped stone implements found there, and someone in Jalisco is also going to send things.
[AB to Tozzer, 14 December ?1909 PM]

After the death of Pablo Solorio, Miss Breton felt that he deserved some recognition for his work in Mexico.

Almost all the small specimens in the cases except those from obsidian workings were collected on the ancient sites by my servant Pablo Solorio, in days of patient search ... In giving any description of my things, I should like full credit awarded to the zeal of P Solorio, as it is an achievement for one man to have made such a collection, often on ploughed land, and always where the things were more or less covered with earth - and he has died recently, a victim to the hardships of camping in Yucatan.
[AB to Quick, 30 January 1905 BCM]

Miss Breton got on well with the director, Dr. H. Bolton, and with his support she hoped that the collections would grow. She offered casts of the doorway of the Upper Temple of the Jaguars, at Chichén Itzá.

I want it to be put up as a door ... I had hoped that you would be able to reserve a part of the new Museum, as an American Court, & that this door could be used as one entrance. I might, in that case, give casts of other notable Central American sculptures which are so strangely lacking in English Museums.
[AB to Bolton, 17 November 1904 BCM]

> Please try to interest Lord Winterstoke [of the Wills tobacco family, who was a benefactor of the Museum] in Central America, and insert a hint as to a Central American Hall ... I am still hoping that my Door may some day be set up.
> [AB to Quick, 30 January 1908 BCM]

Her ideas, though, were on a much larger scale than Bolton's:

> The Bristol Museum should become a headquarters for American archaeology in England. There must be rich men who could take up collecting, or financing expeditions.
> [AB to Bolton, 27 January 1918 BCM]

This grandiose plan was never realised, and the American archaeology collections have not grown substantially since Miss Breton's bequest.

The material in the cases at Bristol was only a small part of the whole collection. Miss Breton's house at Bath was still full, and she left it all to the Museum.

> My late sister, Miss A C Breton ... left a wish that the Art Gallery of the Bristol Museum should have her 'collections' ... I am particularly desirous of a decision in the matter of 10 plaster casts of Maya chieftains [the doorway] which have been in the house for some years preparatory to their being coloured when my sister felt up to doing so.
> [Col Breton to Bolton, 17 November 1923 BCM]

Thus Bristol received:

> All books, journals and literature in general - all drawings and paintings - all objects whether ethnological, geological or curios
> [Col Breton to Bolton, 23 November 1923 BCM]

> In the ethnographical department, the gift of American and other antiquities collected by the late Miss Adela Breton, caused the dismantling of the former Mexican exhibits and the arrangement of a new series of a more detailed character.
> [Annual Report of Bristol Museum and Art Gallery, 1924]

In 1946 an exhibition was mounted of Miss Breton's paintings from the Yucatán. Arranged by the Assistant Curator of Antiquities and Anthropology, G. R. Stanton, the paintings were hung in one of the art galleries(Fig.25). Some of her full-size tracings and copies of the relief at Acancéh and the fresco at Chichén Itzá were shown, the overlapping sections of paper pinned directly to the gallery walls.

In 1952, a selection of her work was exhibited at the International Congress of Americanists, XXX session, held in Cambridge, England. Miss Breton's copies of the wall paintings in the Upper Temple of the Jaguars and all her Caryatid paintings from Chichén Itzá were displayed in company with ancient Mexican manuscripts from the Liverpool Museum, the British Museum and the Bodleian Library.

After this the Breton paintings went unremarked until they were 'rediscovered' in the early 1970s. Sir Eric Thompson and Arthur G. Miller were among the first to see them and realise their importance for modern scholars of ancient Mexico. Miller described the collection as 'an incomparable record ...' (A. Miller 1977: 200).

In 1973, The Museum of Mankind (the Ethnography Department of The British Museum) mounted an exhibition entitled The British and the Maya. This celebrated

25 Photograph of arrangement of paintings for the 1946 exhibition of Adela Breton's paintings, showing the sections of the Acancéh frieze pinned together on the gallery wall. P 3103

the contribution of British explorers, archaeologists and artists to the study of Maya history. Adela Breton's work was included alongside that of such great Meso-Americanists as Alfred Maudslay and Sir Eric Thompson, and her fellow artist Frederick Catherwood.

A small number of her paintings and antiquities were displayed in 1980, as part of the celebrations marking the anniversary of the opening of the Art Gallery and Museum of Antiquities in 1905. Miss Breton had been invited to that opening, but could not attend as:

> 'During the winter I am always good for nothing.'
> [AB to Quick, 30 January 1905 BCM].

In the anniversary exhibition 75 years later, the casts of the doorway were, at last, erected as a door, if only temporarily.

The present exhibition displays a large part of Miss Breton's collections; whilst her work is well-known in America, she is almost unknown in Britain. Yet for the importance of her work to Meso-American studies she deserves to be better known; were it not for her, working in watercolour before the days of colour photography, much would be lost today.

> She was a very remarkable woman
> [Tozzer to Wallis, 18 April 1950 BCM]

Sue Giles

The Paintings

Chichén Itzá

The history of Chichén Itzá is confused and several theories exist to explain it.

The traditional view was that Chichén Itzá was built by the Maya in the Classic period and then invaded by the Toltec in the late 10th century. New theories suggest that the Toltec never occupied the city, though others still support the Toltec influence. Certainly, in about AD 900, Mexican influence appears in the architecture of the site; because similar 'foreign' elements are also found at the Toltec capital of Tula (in central Mexico) this seems to support the Toltec invasion theory. However, these foreign traits may have been introduced into Yucatán by mexicanised Maya groups, perhaps the Putun from the west. Later the site came under the control of a group of mexicanised foreigners called the Itzá, who gave their name to the city.

Whatever the background, the earliest buildings at Chichén Itzá date from the Classic period, built in the Chenes and Puuc styles, with elaborate stone mosaic ornamentation. Before the introduction of foreign cultural elements (in about AD 900) the city was in decline. These contacts brought with them a revival shown in new, hybrid forms of architecture - part Maya, part 'Toltec'. There was no recovery from another decline, beginning in the 13th century: the Itzá were driven out by the Cocom dynasty of the neighbouring city of Mayapán. Chichén Itzá was displaced as the regional centre and abandoned. Mayapán itself was abandoned in the 15th century. When the Spanish arrived in Yucatán in 1528, they found no great centre of authority, as Chichén Itzá had been, but a group of small, independent city states. To avoid confusion, 'Toltec' is used in the catalogue, following the traditional view.

The Church

1 The Church **1902**
Watercolour 610 x 425 mm
Classic (Puuc)

Watercolour of the Church at Chichén Itzá, showing front façade with stone mosaic decoration, including stepped frets, Chac masks or sky serpent masks with stylised hooked noses and *Bacab* masks - also part of the Annexe of the Nunnery with *Chac* mask and sky serpent mask decoration, all overgrown with shrubs.
Ea 8491 *Plate 1*

2 The Annexe of the Nunnery **3.1900**
Watercolour 590 x 420 mm
Classic (Chenes and Puuc)

Watercolour of the east façade of the Annexe of the Nunnery and the Church at Chichén Itzá, showing the Annexe's decoration of *Chac* masks with hooked noses, and a seated figure above the door, and the plainer back of the church (see also Ea 8491), with *Chac* masks on the entablature only.
Note by AB - Casa de Monjas, Chichén Itzá. 3.1900.
Ea 8492 *Plate 4*

Akab Dzib

3 The Akab Dzib
Watercolour 560 x 395 mm
Classic (Puuc)

Watercolour painting of Akab Dzib at Chichén Itzá, showing one end of building range in Puuc style; overgrown with scrub, with moon behind.
Note by AB - Akab Tsib Chichen Itza in which I lived 1900 and 1901.
Ea 8128 *Plate 5*

Sacred Cenote

4 Sceptre from the Sacred Cenote **4.04.2**
Watercolour 254 x 354 mm
Middle Post-Classic (?Toltec-Maya)

Watercolour sketch of four views of kneeling figure sceptre from Sacred Cenote, showing (right side) whole sceptre, with male figure holding ?fan, and chamber within headdress that held burning copal. Front, back and left side views show figure only: (front) headdress and loincloth, with green earstuds, (back) elaborate costume of complex bow and plaited 'mat sign', and (left side) rattle or sceptre held in hand, green colour on knee. Coggins and Shane, 1984: 112, no.123
Note by AB - Sacred Cenote. 1/1. This had a gold mask over face.
Ea 8218 *Plate 6*

5 Sceptre from the Sacred Cenote
Watercolour 290 x 515 mm
Middle Post-Classic

Watercolour painting of three views of diving figure sceptre from Sacred Cenote, showing (front) whole sceptre with jade mosaic covering face, large bow on forehead, simple collar and large earstuds, holding balls of ?copal. Side and back views show figure only, back view showing lattice work of chamber between legs which may have held burning copal. Scale 1/1.
Coggins and Shane, 1984: 113, No.125 (catalogue photograph shows sceptre has cracked and warped since AB painted it wet from Cenote).
Note by AB - Dredged from Sacred Cenote. May 1904. 5 sheets.
Ea 11013

Ball Court

6 The Ball Court
Photographs 204 x 150 mm
Post-Classic (Toltec-Maya)

Biol.Cent.Am. Part XIII pl.28. Photographs (by H.Sweet) showing the Ball Court as it was when Maudslay first worked there, 1888-89, with the encroaching jungle cleared. Top looking N, bottom looking S. (Maudslay, 1899: 193-211)
Ea 8213

7 Ball Court Ring
Pencil and watercolour 175 x 155 mm
Post-Classic (Toltec-Maya)

Pencil and watercolour sketch of stone ring from west wall of Ball Court, showing carved surface with two interlaced feathered serpents coiled around ring.
Ea 11030b

Upper Temple of the Jaguars

8 Warrior Figure K4
Watercolour 570 x 110 mm
Post-Classic (Toltec-Maya)

Watercolour of warrior figure K4 from door jambs. Name above head is Rodent: wears standard uniform of Toltec officers, fringed sleeve on left arm with hafted stone point tucked into top, fur or feather bands on wrist and legs, back disc or shield tied around waist and mosaic-covered pill box hat with winged ornament and two white feathers, with collar of strung stone blades and multistrand jade bead necklace; carries *atlatl* with fur pieces attached, curved fending stick, spears and bag.
Scale 1/4.
Ea 8438 *Plate 7*

9 Warrior Figure K9
Watercolour 570 x 105 mm
Post-Classic (Toltec-Maya)

Watercolour of warrior figure K9 from door jambs. Name above head is Snake: wears flounced or padded protective sleeve on right arm with hafted stone point tucked into top, back disc or shield tied around waist and fur or feather bands on left arm and legs, and mosaic-covered pill box hat with two white feathers, with square-cut bead collars; carries *atlatl*, bag and spears.
Scale 1/4.
Ea 8439 *Plate 7*

10 Warrior Figure K4 **1907**
Pencil drawing 570 x 110 mm
Post-Classic (Toltec-Maya)

Pencil drawing by Col.H.d'Arch Breton of warrior figure K4 from door jamb. Measured drawing made from casts.
Scale 1/4.
Ea 8441

11 Warrior Figure K9 **1907**
Pencil drawing 570 x 110 mm
Post-Classic (Toltec-Maya)

Pencil drawing by Col.H.d'Arch Breton of warrior figure K9 from door jamb. Measured drawing made from casts.
Scale 1/4.
Ea 8443

Upper Temple of the Jaguars - Outer Chamber

12 Caryatid II
Watercolour 560 x 385 mm
Post-Classic (Toltec-Maya)

Watercolour of three views of Caryatid II. Atlantean figure wearing (front) green, red and yellow headdress, red loincloth/kilt, red knee and ankle bands and sandals, with green bracelets, earstuds, jaguar pectoral and collar and (back) cloak of yellow and green curved feathers, with red and green neck edge and a side view of figure.
Note by AB - green side feathers ? [green feathers on right side only].
Ea 8189IIa *Plate 8*

13 Caryatid III
Watercolour 325 x 510 mm
Post-Classic (Toltec-Maya)

Watercolour of front view of Caryatid III. Atlantean figure wearing green and white headdress, white fringed green loincloth or kilt with fawn ?belt with roundel, knee and ankle bands and sandals, with green bracelets, elaborate square earstuds, butterfly pectoral, mulitistrand necklace and nosestud.
Scale 1/2.
Note by AB - Height 37+ in. Width on top [-]
Ea 8189IIIa *Plate 9*

14 Caryatid III
Watercolour 250 x 355 mm
Post-Classic (Toltec-Maya)

Watercolour of front view of Caryatid III. As Ea 8189IIIa but with pale green belt, not fawn.
Scale 1/3.
Ea 8189IIIb

15 Caryatid IV
Watercolour 560 x 394 mm
Post-Classic (Toltec-Maya)

Watercolour of three views of Caryatid IV. Atlantean figure wearing (front) green and white headdress, red loincloth/kilt, red knee and ankle bands, with green bracelets, earstuds, butterfly pectoral and collar, with green and white nosestuds, and (back) cloak of yellow and green curved feathers with red and blue neck edge, and a side view of figure.
Ea 8189IVb *Plate 10*

16 Caryatid VI
Watercolour 360 x 510 mm
Post-Classic (Toltec-Maya)

Watercolour of front view of Caryatid VI. Atlantean figure, wearing white headdress with red feathers, body paint, white bow, red leg bands (or lower edge of kilt?) and sandals, with green bracelets, red and yellow earstuds and round yellow pectoral on bead necklace.
Ea 8189VIa *Plate 12*

17 Caryatid VIII
Watercolour 340 x 360 mm
Post-Classic (Toltec-Maya)

Watercolour of front and rear views of Caryatid VIII. Atlantean figure wearing (front) red and white hat with red feathers, red loincloth/kilt, red knee and ankle bands and sandals, with green bracelets, earstuds and collar, with nosestud, and (back) cloak of green straight and curved feathers with red and yellow neck edge.
Ea 8189VIIIa *Plate 13*

18 Caryatids VIII & IX
Watercolour 320 x 350 mm
Post-Classic (Toltec-Maya)

Watercolour of side views of Caryatids VIII and IX. Atlantean figures, facing right, wearing red kilts and accessories with green jewellery, and green feather cloaks.
Ea 8189VIIIb

19 Caryatid IX
Watercolour 557 x 390 mm
Post-Classic (Toltec-Maya)

Watercolour of three views of Caryatid IX. Atlantean figure wearing (front) green and white headdress, red loincloth, red knee and ankle bands, with green bracelets, earstuds, square collar and nosestud, (back) green feather cloak (some feathers curved) with red and yellow neck edge - also side view of complete figure.
Ea 8189IXb *Plate 11*

20 Caryatid XI
Watercolour 247 x 300 mm
Post-Classic (Toltec-Maya)

Watercolour of front and side views of Caryatid XI. Atlantean figure wearing (front), white cap and green loincloth/kilt wrapped around neck, and sandals, with one white bracelet, yellow and red feather neck ties of cloak, white and yellow knee and ankle bands, and (back), cloak of white feathers with red neck band.
Note by AB - note if tips coloured [of cloak].
Ea 8189XI *Plate 14*

21 Caryatids in Situ **1903**
Photograph 270 x 200 mm
Post-Classic (Toltec-Maya)

Photograph of Caryatids V, XV and X (foreground figures).
Note by AB - Front figures that supported table.
Ea 11073c

22 Caryatids in Situ
Photograph with watercolour detail 255 x 200 mm
Post-Classic (Toltec-Maya)

Photograph of Caryatids I, II, III, IV, V and IX with watercolour detail added, showing five figures in detail, also door jambs.
Note by AB - Side row of the altar statues.Temple A.
Ea 11074a *Plate 15*

23 Altar Table
Watercolour 775 x 570 mm
Post-Classic (Toltec-Maya)

Watercolour sketch of altar table from Upper Temple of the Jaguars, showing part of bottom left and right quadrants, with (left) part of seated figure of Toltec warrior, with flounced or padded protective sleeve on left arm, fur or feather bands on right arm, legs and ankles, waist shield and sandals, and carrying *atlatl* and curved fending stick; (right), feet of warrior, wearing fur or feather ankle bands and sandals, with points of three downward-pointing spears; body of feathered serpent behind; seated Toltec warriors around edge.
Scale 1/3.
Notes by AB in margins.
Ea 12307 *Plate 18*

Upper Temple of the Jaguars - Inner Chamber

24 Fresco **1903**
Watercolour 658 x 907 mm
Post-Classic (Toltec-Maya)

Watercolour copy of wall painting on south wall of Upper Temple of the Jaguars, showing a battle scene: the fighting takes place near a lake town on hilly ground, hence the use of wooden siege towers and ladders. At the bottom, officers sit in camp, with prisoners brought before them. [There are different interpretations of this series of frescos: for example, Coggins (Coggins 1984) explains this as the last narrative scene of the story of the Toltec victory over the Maya and other non-Mexican people. The scene takes place at night, the end of a daily Sun cycle, and three celestial serpent warriors above the village oversee the fighting. At the right, the Venus warrior (representing the Toltec) riding a feathered serpent leads the Sun Disc (representing the Maya), thus symbolising the Toltec victory over the Maya. Miller (A. Miller 1977) interprets the frescos as two separate groups, the south group showing two invasions of Seibal in Guatemala by the Itzá Captain Sun Disc and the Putun-Itzá Captain Serpent, and the North group showing an attack on a village outside the Maya area, possibly in Oaxaca, with Captain Sun Disc and Captain Serpent fighting on opposite sides].
Ea 8482 *Plate 19*

25 Fresco
Watercolour 715 x 850 mm
Post-Classic (Toltec-Maya)

Watercolour copy of wall painting on south end of west wall of Upper Temple of the Jaguars, showing a scene after battle; a town has been captured, and the victorious troops perform a war dance or military drill. At the bottom, the officers sit in camp before their temporary ?thatch huts, receiving petitioners who sit with their arms across their chests.
[There are different interpretations of this series of frescos: for example, Coggins (Coggins 1984) explains this as one scene in the story of the Toltec victory over the Maya and other non-Mexican peoples. Here, the Toltecs have taken the town and the Sun Disc: at the right Quetzalcoatl, protected by a green feathered serpent, and Mixcoatl, with mosaic-covered serpent, arrive, the two legendary conquerors of Chichén Itzá. Miller (A. Miller 1977) interprets the frescos as two separate groups, the South showing two invasions of Seibal in Guatemala by the Itzá Captain Sun Disc and the Putun-Itzá Captain Serpent, and the North showing a military campaign outside the Maya area, probably in Oaxaca. This section shows the fighting troops of Captain Serpent and their capabilities, following the conquest of a town].
1/4 scale
Ea 8481

26 Fresco
Line block with watercolour detail 594 x 355 mm
Post Classic (Toltec-Maya)

Line block with watercolour detail of fresco of south vault of the Upper Temple of the Jaguars, showing warriors and, in lower register, a heart sacrifice, with the victim held hand and foot, and watched over by a feathered serpent.
Ea 10951 *Plate 20*

Lower Temple of the Jaguars

27 West Wall Relief **1909**
Photograph with watercolour detail 614 x 482 mm
Post-Classic (Toltec-Maya)

Photograph of west wall of Lower Temple of the Jaguars with the figures outlined in watercolour or ink, showing three registers of carved figures; upper register with elaborately dressed Toltec warriors, each holding a bunch of spears, centre with elaborately dressed personages holding staves, making offerings to masked figure, and lower with elaborately dressed warriors carying one spear. Feathered serpent surrounds central masked figure, focus of attention.
Note by AB - Chamber E. Temple of the Tigers, Chichén Itzá. From a photo by T. Maler, and plates A. Maudslay.
Ea 8493 *Plate 21*

Teotihuacán

The great city of Teotihuacán was founded in the late Pre-Classic period: growth was rapid, and at its peak in the early Classic, it was a magnificent civic and religious centre, carefully planned and laid out along a main avenue. The influence of Teotihuacán was extended as far as Guatemala and Honduras. A slow decline thereafter ended in about AD 750 when Teotihuacán was partially destroyed by unknown invaders, and squatters moved into the remains. What lay behind the decline and invasion is not known. Theories include: long-term economic problems which disrupted trade and tribute; political discontent; or ecological disasters caused by natural climatic changes or by deforestation (for the building of the city) which caused soil erosion and consequent changes in climate and productivity of the land. The builders of this great city are unknown: Nahua, Totonac, Otomi and Popoloca peoples have all been suggested, but there is no strong evidence. Native tradition held that it was built by giants or gods, and even Aztec rulers made pilgrimage on foot to this great site.

Teopancaxco

28 Pulque Priests Mural
Watercolour 2980 x 790 mm
Classic

Watercolour of the Pulque Priests mural from the south wall of the inner room of Casa de Barrios at Teopancaxco, showing two priests facing a central shrine-like motif; at each end is a vertical flower band; the priest on the left is roughly sketched, in yellow, pink and red, with several unpainted areas, showing elaborate headdress and costume, a 'flowery' speech scroll, and a libation with pendant flowers and central motif, showing a disc with rays, with red, pink and green interlace filling; priest on the right is more fully drawn and painted, in yellow, green, pink and red, showing elaborate headdress and costume, a ceremonial bag, and 'flowery' speech scroll and libation without pendant flowers.
Ea 8360 *Plate 22* - not in exhibition

29 Pulque Priests Mural
Watercolour 910 x 756 mm
Classic

Watercolour of mural from wall of outer room of Casa de Barrios at Teopancaxco, showing a priest, facing right, wearing elaborate clothing and headdress: he carries a ceremonial bag, scatters seed and chants a prayer. Painted in bright colours, green, yellow, pink and red, with red background colour.
Note by AB - Beyond door in antechamber 9?
Ea 8362 *Plate 23* - not in exhibition

30 Armed Figure
Watercolour 190 x 180 mm
Classic

Watercolour sketch of armed figure from Casa de Barrios at Teopancaxco, showing warrior figure from procession on wall. Pen and ink sketches of libations in margins.
Note by AB - From Peñafiel. Coloured on spot from the fresco said to have been copied from the original by a former owner of the house, on a thick piece of stucco cut out of an ancient wall. This end/ in Peñafiel/ is not there now. at a house. loose.
Ea 8265 *Plate 24* - not in exhibition

Acancéh

The town of Acancéh is built upon, and using the stones of, the pre-Hispanic structure of the Classic period site. The Palace of the Stuccoes, although in poor condition, is a unique building, the front façade being decorated with painted stucco relief. The relief was covered in antiquity by a new building, and uncovered in 1906 when the stones of the new building were quarried for re-use. Exposure of the stucco frieze has led to damage by rain, so that the coloured paintings by Adela Breton are an extremely important record of what was a brilliant, dazzling work of art.

31 Acancéh Frieze
Watercolour 670 x 1331 mm
Classic

Watercolour of bird from the east end of the frieze, facing outwards, showing (a) the body and leg and claws of a large raptorial bird; the oval body is a blank space, the leg painted ?brown or ?pink, with red background, and (b) the wing and part of a claw of a large raptorial bird; the wing outlined in blue with red patterning and pendant yellow and green feathers. Notes by AB in margins.
Ea 8220a-b - not in exhibition

32 Acancéh Frieze, Panels 1 to 5
Watercolour 2800 x 1500 mm
Classic

Watercolour of section of Acancéh frieze, showing panels 1 to 5, within stepped frames, with red background colour. Panel 1, seated anthropomorphised ?jaguar; 2, lower half of a bird; 3, seated squirrel; 4, wings of a bird, an ?eagle; 5, part of the head of an animal.
Ea 8186b - not in exhibition

33 Acancéh Frieze, Panels 6 to 11
Watercolour 2760 x 1190 mm
Classic

Watercolour of section of the Acancéh frieze, showing panels 6 to 11, within stepped frames, with red background colour. Panel 6 blank, save for three green feathers and a speech scroll; 7, blank save for part of a ?headdress; 8, anthropomorphised bat, painted brown; 9, seated animal or God N, a god of the underworld, with blue body; 10, bird or bat, painted blue and shades of red; 11, serpent. [Panel 11 completely, and panels 9 and 10 partly, destroyed before 1930 by the removal of stones for building use.])
Ea 8186a *Plate 25* – not in exhibition

34 Acancéh Frieze, Panels 17 to 21
Watercolour 2130 x 1100 mm
Classic

Watercolour of section of Acancéh frieze, showing panels 17 to 21, within stepped frames, with red background colour. Panel 17, tail of seated ?jaguar; 18, part of Quetzal bird, with long green tail feathers; 19, seated opossum, painted yellow; 20, monkey; 21, serpent, rattlesnake, painted yellow and blue.
Ea 10975 - not in exhibition

35 Acancéh Frieze
Watercolour 2487 x 416 mm
Classic

Watercolour of the upper border of the frieze, showing a stylised eye and drop of water falling from a blue border.
[This upper border symbolises water falling from the sky, rain given as a gift from a god.]
Ea 8186c. *Plate 26* - not in exhibition

Aké

Aké was first settled probably in the Classic period, but declined in importance over time. At the time of the Spanish Conquest, it was still occupied, and the new colonists aided the ruin of the old ceremonial buildings: the ruins of Aké were incorporated into a *hacienda.*

36 The Katunes of Aké **1.1901**
Watercolour 517 x 285 mm
Classic

Watercolour sketch of Katunes of Aké, or the Colonnaded Building, showing remains of pyramid or platform base with stone-built columns on top, all overgrown with low scrub.
Ea 8221 *Plate 27*

Cempoala

Cempoala flourished throughout the Post-Classic period; it was under Aztec control when Cortés and his Spanish troops landed. The buildings were covered in burnished plaster, which the Spanish at first thought was silver. The archaeological site is still well preserved, with the remains of a city wall and a large ceremonial complex with pyramids and temples.

37 Ruins of Cempoala
Watercolour 397 x 510 mm
Late Post-Classic (?Aztec)

Watercolour of ruins at Cempoala, showing part of pyramid or platform base, in two terraces, with central stairway; all overgrown with large trees growing from top. Note by Stanton - Probably Casa de Moctezuma.
Ea 8356

38 Ruins of Cempoala **1.95**
Watercolour 510 x 275 mm
Late Post-Classic (?Aztec)

Watercolour sketch of ruins at Cempoala, showing part of pyramid or plaform base, in three terraces, with wide central stairway; all overgrown with trees and shrubs.
Ea 8357 *Plate 28*

El Tajín

El Tajín is the most important Veracruz site of the Classic period. The area is now occupied by the Totonac people, but whether it was they or an unknown group who built this centre is not known. El Tajín is a vast site, although the main buildings are concentrated within a small area. Many of the structures have never been excavated, and some that were excavated have been engulfed again by the rain-forest. El Tajín was burnt and abandoned about AD 1200: according to tradition it was destroyed by a *Chichimeca* group.

39 Pyramid of the Niches
Watercolour 340 x 510 mm
Classic

Watercolour of the Pyramid of the Niches at El Tajín, showing the stairway and part of the terracing with niches, all overgrown.
Note by AB - stairway of El Tajín, Papantla.
Ea 8125 *Plate 29*

40 Pyramid of the Niches **1894**
Watercolour 597 x 442 mm
Classic

Watercolour painting of the Pyramid of the Niches at El Tajín, showing the central stairway; all overgrown with scrub, with fallen carved stones in foreground.
Ea 8144 *Plate 31*

Etzatlán

Mound of Guadalupe

Adela Breton was present at the 'excavation' of a burial mound in 1896. This particular mound belonged to a *hacienda* and the owner opened it for amusement; many of the western Mexico mounds and shaft tombs were opened by their owners, or looted by tomb robbers who could sell the contents. The Guadalupe mound was about 40 feet high, with one burial near the centre.

41 Female Figure
Watercolour 380 x 585 mm
Pre-Classic or Classic (Jalisco)

Watercolour of Jalisco figure from Mound of Guadalupe, showing front view of standing female figure holding bowl to left shoulder, wearing ?skirt, with tattooed or painted face, breasts and stomach, and wearing bracelets, nose rings and multiple earrings (Ea 8100). On reverse, unfinished watercolour sketch of mountains.
Note by AB - From Mound. Hacienda of Guadalupe, Etzatlán clay figure. Same size. 18 in.
Published Breton, 1903
Ea 8251a *Plate 32*

42 Female Figure
Watercolour 177 x 253 mm
Pre-Classic or Classic (Jalisco)

Watercolour sketch of Jalisco figure from Mound of Guadalupe, showing side view of standing female figure with sloping forehead, very thick legs and scarification on upper arms (E 5103).
Note by AB - Mound of Guadalupe. 12 inches high, [-] in. thick. Hollow. Has been covered with red glaze upon which are traces of white.
Published Breton, 1903.
Ea 8251c *Plate 33*

43 Male Figure **5.5.96**
Watercolour 177 x 253 mm
Pre-Classic or Classic

Watercolour sketch of ceramic figure from Mound of Guadalupe, showing front view of male figure, arms and legs broken, wearing loincloth, necklace and bandolier, multiple earrings, nose ring and head band, with tattooing or body painting on chest. On back, profile view of head of figure.
Note by AB - from Mound. Hacienda of Guadalupe.
Published Breton, 1903.
Ea 8251e *Plate 34*

44 Ceramic Bowl **5.5.96**
Watercolour 177 x 253 mm
Pre-Classic or Classic (Nayarit)

Watercolour sketch of bowl from Mound of Guadalupe, showing narrow rimmed shallow bowl, with geometric pattern on top

shoulder in red and yellow and random hatched pattern on base in shades of buff. E 5067.
Note by AB - Bowl from Mound of Guadalupe. 1/1.
Published Breton, 1903.
Ea 8251f

Mitla

The site of Mitla was first occupied during the Pre-Classic period; the palace complexes were built in the early Post-Classic period, following the abandonment of Monte Albán, the main Classic centre of the Oaxaca area. The buildings at Mitla are very beautiful, arranged around courtyards, and decorated inside and out with stone mosaic. The designs of the mosaic decoration may derive from woven fabrics, and originally would have been set against the dark red stucco of the wall, where today the colours are all stone. At the time of the conquest, Mitla was the residence of the Zapotec high priest, though the architecture and frescos at the site show strong Mixtec influence.

Palace of the Columns

45 The Palace of the Columns
Watercolour 393 x 205 mm
Post-Classic (Zapotec/Mixtec)

Watercolour sketch of courtyard of Palace of the Columns at Mitla, showing remains of wall from steps of now restored area, with doorway with mosaic lintel, parts of wall and two columns behind - Pablo sitting beside fallen lintel.
Note by AB - Ancient Palace, Mitla.
Ea 8279 *Plate 35*

46 The Palace of the Columns
Watercolour 390 x 305 mm
Post-Classic (Zapotec/Mixtec)

Watercolour view of the ruins at Mitla, showing the Palace of Columns. View through a doorway across the courtyard, with red-painted stucco visible on doorways.
Ea 8277 *Plate 37*

Uxmal

Like most of the great sites, Uxmal developed over the centuries from a small village settlement into a political, religious and administrative centre. The main buildings date from the Classic period: the House of the Magician was said to have been built in one night by a dwarf magician. The architectural style is mainly Puuc, characterised by the mosaic masonry decoration, elegant proportions and fine stone veneer. As with other Maya sites, there was a decline and collapse about AD 900: the cause or causes may have been political, economic or ecological, but Uxmal was no longer the regional centre.

47 The Pyramid of the Magician
Watercolour 425 x 605 mm
Late Classic (Puuc/Chenes style)

Watercolour of the Pyramid of the Magician at Uxmal, showing the west façade from the Nunnery Quadrangle, with stone mosaic decoration of entrance and walls - the doorway representing a mouth within a mask.
Ea 8123 *Plate 38*

48 The Nunnery Quadrangle
Watercolour 255 x 360 mm
Late Classic (Puuc style)

Watercolour sketch of the Nunnery Quadrangle at Uxmal, showing the decoration above the doorways and plain lower walls, of fretwork, false columns and thatched huts.
Ea 8224 *Plate 39*

Xochicalco

Xochicalco is a complicated site. A late Classic ceremonial centre, it seems to link the earlier culture of Teotihuacán with the later one of the Toltecs. Xochicalco gained in importance as Teotihuacán declined, and like Teotihuacán little is known of the people who built it and lived there. There was obviously strong influence from many other peoples: the main building is the Temple of the Feathered Serpent where the feathered serpent of highland Mexico is combined with seated figures in Maya style, with other elements which seem to derive from El Tajín and the cultures of Oaxaca. The site shows a hybrid culture, but in the context of the turbulent ninth century AD, it is not clear who was dominant.

49 The Temple of the Feathered Serpent
Watercolour 815 x 140 mm
Late Classic

Watercolour sketch of east wall of the Temple of the Feathered Serpent at Xochicalco, showing the two feathered serpents, with seated figures and glyphs in undulations of body. Feathers painted green, outline of body yellow, blue water symbols (as interpreted by AB in Breton, 1906) and red background colour.
Note by AB - Xochicalco. east side. Drawn from photographs coloured from reliefs at Chichén Itzá and other sources. Doubtful parts left white.
Ea 8273b *Plate 40*

Mexico City

The Aztecs founded their capital, Tenochtitlan, in about AD 1345, on islands in the 'Lake of the Moon': this was the place where the tribal prophecy was fulfilled, that a city should be built where an eagle was seen on a cactus with a snake in its mouth. The city was enlarged with 'floating gardens' (that is, reclaimed swampland), and by drainage, and as Aztec power grew it became the centre of the empire. The Spanish found in 1519 a well-ordered, stone-built city of 300,000 people, which they compared to Venice.

50 Maguey Plan of Tenochtitlan **1908**
Watercolour 1680 x 990 mm
Post-Classic (Aztec) - Colonial

Pen and ink and watercolour copy of part of the Maguey Plan of western suburb of Tenochtitlan, present-day Mexico City; showing *chinampas* or 'floating gardens', causeways and canals of the area, with houses and inhabitants shown; Christian churches and Spanish glosses added later (before 1562). Copy of map made at request of A.P.Maudslay for publication with his translation of Bernal Diaz del Castillo (see Breton, 1910).
Ea 8367a *Plate 41* - not in exhibition

Cholula

51 Great Pyramid and Church, Cholula **1892**
Watercolour 565 x 395 mm
Classic and Colonial

Watercolour painting of church and pyramid at Cholula, showing remains of overgrown Great Pyramid with colonial period church of Nuestra Señora de los Remedios built on top.
Ea 8145 *Plate 42*

Texcoco

52 Stone Statue
Watercolour 505 x 340 mm

Watercolour sketch of fallen statue near Texcoco, showing a huge, square-cut stone figure of a goddess lying in scrub, with Pablo sitting beside it.
Note by AB - Tecomate [?] near Texcoco. Headdress. Nose. Teeth. Foot.
Ea 8267

Itzamal

53 Stucco Relief
Watercolour 340 x 507 mm

Watercolour sketch of house wall at Itzamal, showing reused stucco relief in wall, with indistinct kneeling male figure.
Ea 8358

San Andres Chalchicomula

54 Old House **1894**
Watercolour 265 x 340 mm

Watercolour sketch of old house in San Andres Chalchicomula, showing courtyard of house in ruinous state, with upper walls fallen down, roof off and part of verandah roof fallen in, two children and a turkey in yard.
Ea 8403 *Plate 43*

55 View of San Andres Chalchicomula **1894**
Watercolour 340 x 510 mm

Watercolour sketch of San Andres Chalchicomula, showing view from path above town, through a bridge, with church dominating town and mountains in background.
Ea 8401 *Plate 44*

56 Volcano of Orizaba
Watercolour 245 x 340 mm

Watercolour view of volcano of Orizaba from San Andres Chalchicomula, with maize fields in foreground and church in middle ground, mountains and volcano in background. On reverse, watercolour sketches of women and children.
Ea 8404

Aguascalientes

57 Cathedral of Aguascalientes **1896(?)**
Watercolour 385 x 560 mm

Watercolour sketch of cathedral at Aguascalientes, showing elaborately carved façade, in front two women on knees. Painted from photograph? Unfinished.
Ea 8148 *Plate 45*

Guanajuato

58 View of Guanajuato
Watercolour 510 x 340 mm

Watercolour sketch of view near Guanajuato, from hillside overlooking town, showing town with prominent church, surrounding fields and mountains, with plain in background between two mountain ranges.
Ea 8389

Ixtacamaxtitlan

59 View of Ixtacamaxtitlan
Watercolour 390 x 565 mm

Watercolour sketch of view near Ixtacamaxtitlan, showing dry riverbed in foreground, with arid looking fields - mountains and volcanic plugs in background.
Ea 8402

Meztitlan

60 View of Church Enclosure, Meztitlan
Watercolour sketch 340 x 240 mm

Watercolour view of church enclosure at Metztitlan, showing wall around enclosure, roofs of houses outside, cacti forest on hillside, mountains in background.
Ea 8407

Tlacotepec

61 View of Volcanoes from Tlacotepec **January 1898**
Watercolour 560 x 390 mm

Watercolour sketch of view from Tlacotepec, showing trees and scrub in foreground and mountain ranges stretching into background.
Note by AB - near Tlacotepec, Guerrero. Looking over valley of las Biloas, towards the volcanoes of Toluca, Popocatepetl and Ixtaccihuatl. Oaks, evergreen and otherwise. [i.e. deciduous.]
Ea 8380

Tlaxcala

62 View of Tlaxcala **1894**
Watercolour sketch 340 x 360 mm

Watercolour sketch of view of Tlaxcala from hillside in town, showing flat- roofed houses with church dominating, fields and trees with another church and town in distance and mountains in background.
Ea 8406 *Plate 46*

Chapala

63 Jalisco Figure **1896**
Watercolour 290 x 505 mm
Classic

Painting of Jalisco ceramic figure with decorated breasts. Front view, showingkneeling female holding bowl on left shoulder. Note by AB - Dug up at Chapala, Jalisco. May 1896. Painted clay. 1/1.
Ea 8245a

Otumba

64 Stone Statues
Watercolour 505 x 340 mm

Watercolour sketch of three statues from Otumba, showing square-cut figures, one ?female, with headdress and skirts or kilts, with hands held in front of stomach, the two men perhaps holding objects in hands.
Note by AB - Chicacoatl [below one of the figures]. In garden, Otumba. from S.Martin (near Teotihuacan).
Ea 8268b

Site Unknown

65 Market Place
Watercolour 250 x 175 mm

Watercolour sketch of market in unknown place, showing pottery stall in foreground and other stalls in background around edge of plaza, under white umbrellas.
Ea 8422 *Plate 47*

26 Photograph taken by Adela Breton of the market in an unidentified town. Ea 8444

1 View of the front façade of the Church at Chichén Itzá and also part of the Annexe of the Nunnery Ea 8491, Cat.No.1

2 (*above*) Photograph of the front façade of the Church at Chichén Itzá and also part of the Annexe of The Nunnery, May 1989
3 (*below*) Photograph of Akab Dzib at Chichén Itzá, May 1989

4 View of the east façade of the Annexe of the Nunnery and also the Church at Chichén Itzá Ea 8492, Cat.No.2

5 View of Akab Dzib at Chichén Itzá, built in the Puuc style Ea 8128, Cat.No.3

6 Four views of the kneeling figure sceptre from the Sacred Cenote at Chichén Itzá Ea 8218, Cat.No.4

7 Warrior figures K4 and K9 from the door jambs of the Upper Temple of the Jaguars at Chichén Itzá Ea 8438 and Ea 8439, Cat.Nos.8 and 9

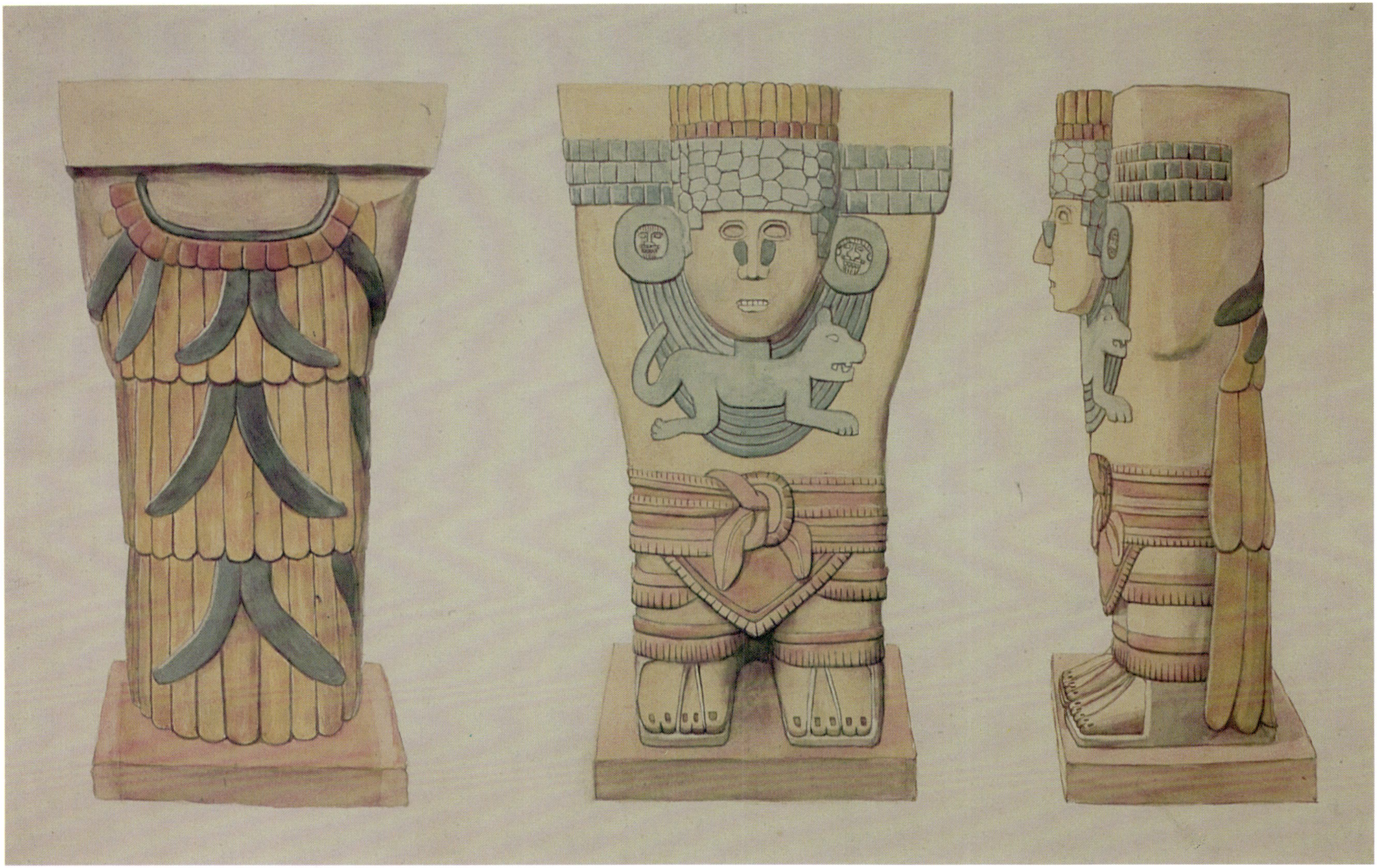

8 Three views of Caryatid II from the Outer Chamber of the Upper Temple of the Jaguars, Chichén Itzá Ea 8189IIa, Cat.No.12

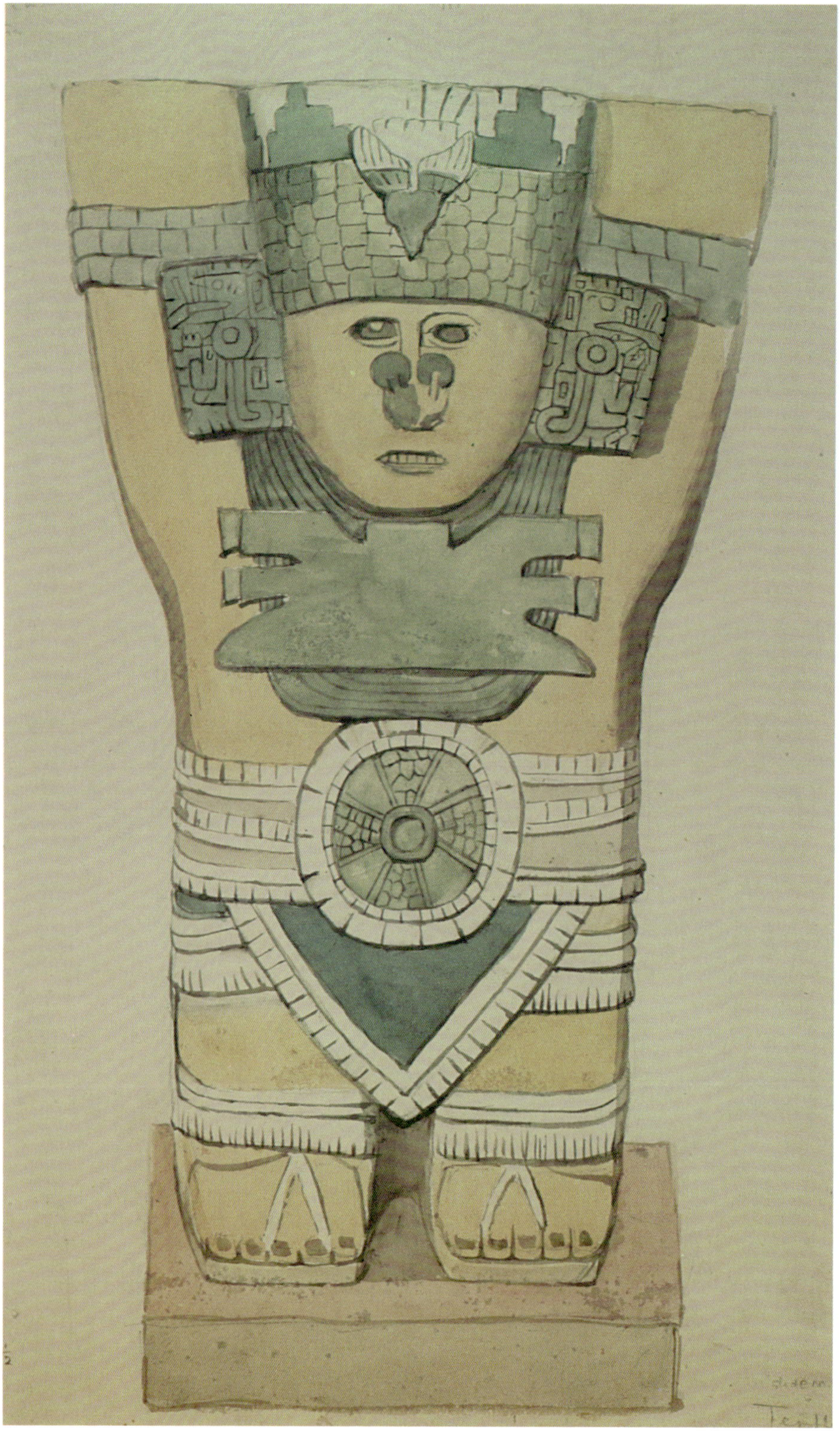

9 Front view of Caryatid III Ea 8189IIIa, Cat.No.13

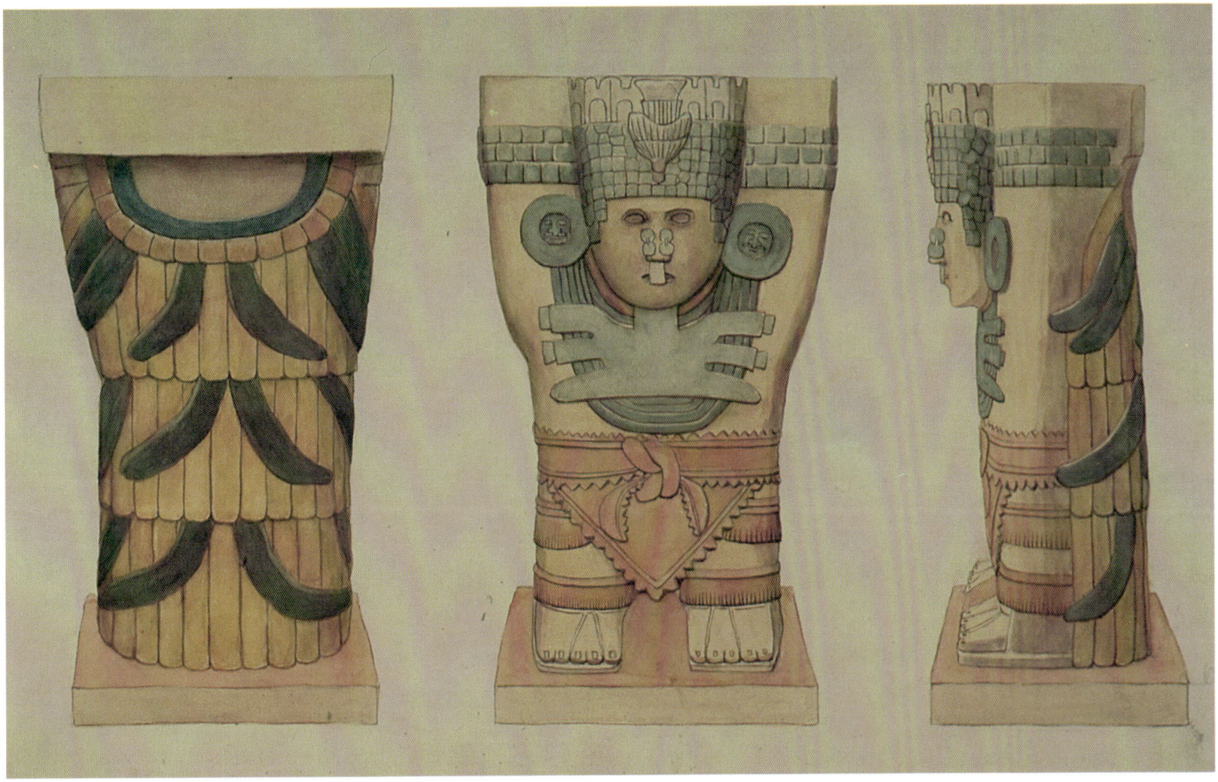

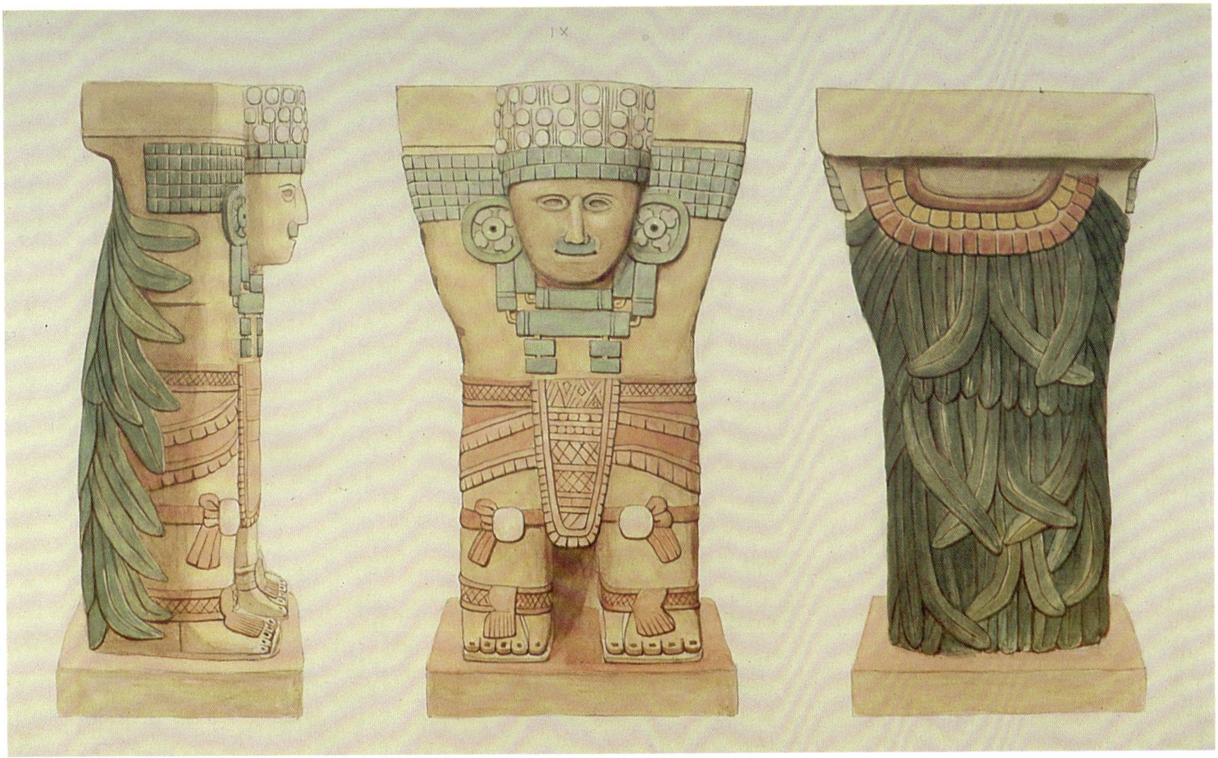

10 (*above*) Three views of Caryatid IV Ea 8189IVb, Cat.No.15
11 (*below*) Three views of Caryatid IX Ea 8189IXb, Cat.No.19

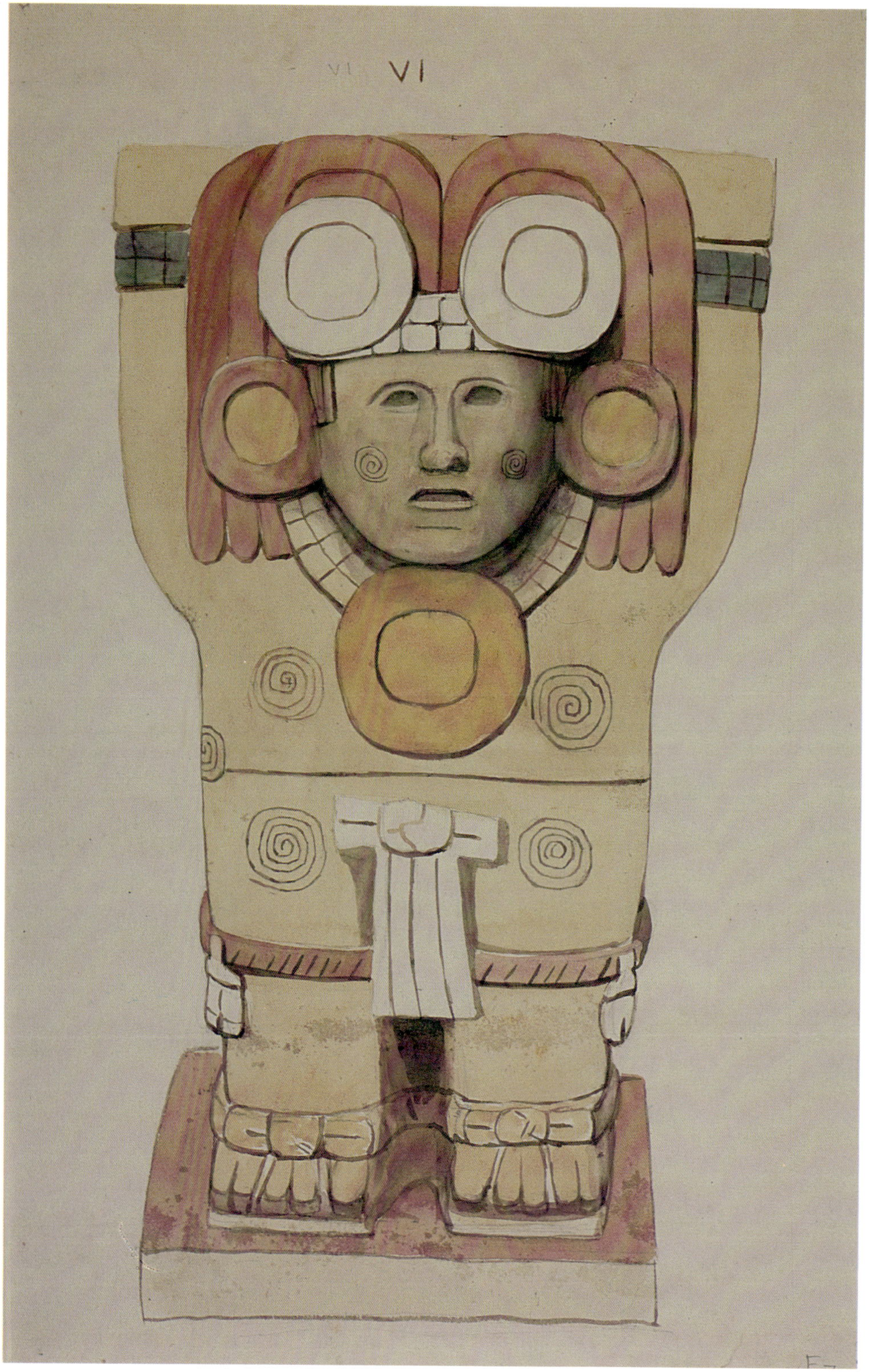

12 Front view of Caryatid VI Ea 8189VIa, Cat.No.16

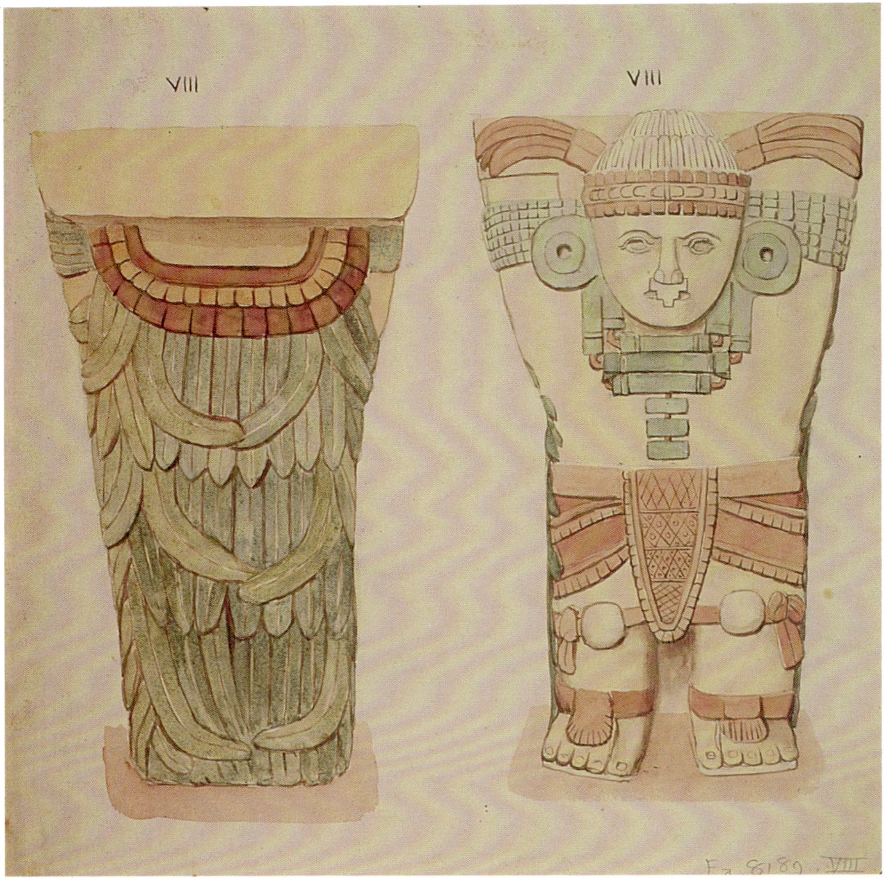

13 Front and rear views of Caryatid VIII Ea 8189VIIIa, Cat.No.17

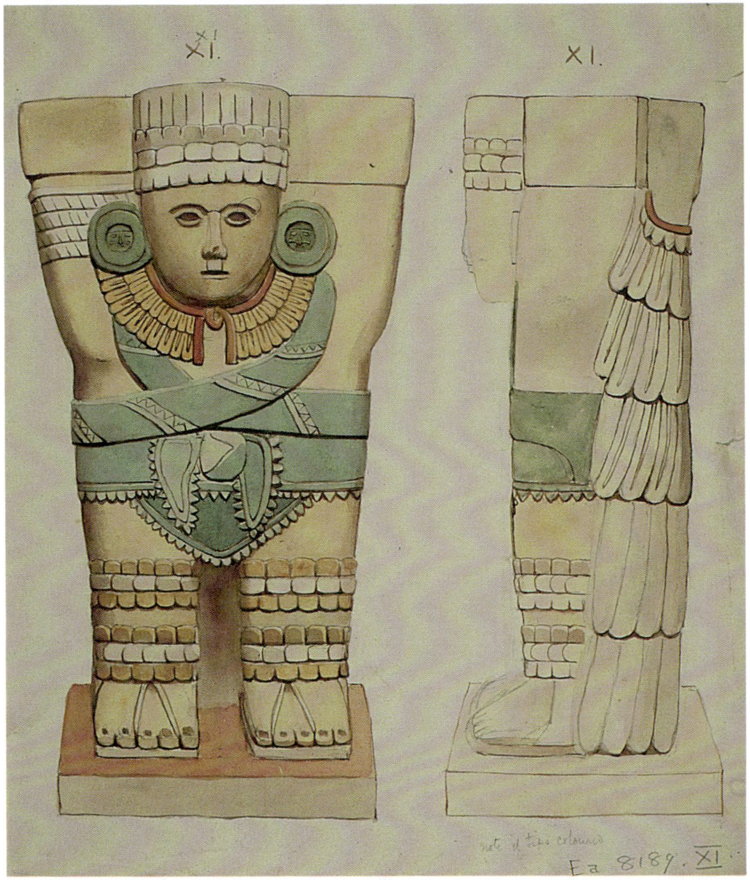

14 Front and side views of Caryatid XI Ea 8189XI, Cat.No.20

15 (*above*) View of Caryatids I, II, III, V and IX *in situ* also showing the door jambs of the Upper Temple of the Jaguars Ea 11074c, Cat.No.22
16 (*below*) Caryatids from the Upper Temple of the Jaguars on display at the National Museum, Mexico City, May 1989

17 *(above)* Photograph of the altar table from the Temple of the Warriors, Chichén Itzá, May 1989
18 *(below)* Sketch of part of the altar table from the Upper Temple of the Jaguars, Chichén Itzá Ea 12307, Cat.No.23

19 Copy of the battle scene on the south wall of the Upper Temple of the Jaguars, Chichén Itzá Ea 8482, Cat.No.24

20 Detail of the fresco of the South Vault of the Upper Temple of the Jaguars, Chichén Itzá Ea 10951, Cat.No.26

21 View of carved figures on the west wall of the Lower Temple of the Jaguars, Chichén Itzá Ea 8493, Cat.No.27

22 Copy of a detail from the Pulque Priests mural from Casa de Barrios, Teopancaxco Ea 8360, Cat.No.28

23 Copy of a mural from Casa de Barrios, Teopancaxco, showing a priest. Ea 8362, Cat.No.29

24 Copy of a figurine from the outer chamber at Teopancaxco. Ea 8265, Cat.No.30

25 Copy of panels 6 to 11 of the Acancéh frieze Ea 8186a, Cat.No.33

26 Copy of the upper border of the Acancéh frieze Ea 8186c, Cat.No.35

27 View of the Katunes of Aké or Colonnaded Building Ea 8221, Cat.No.36

28 Sketch of the ruins at Cempoala Ea 8357, Cat.No.38

29 View of the Pyramid of the Niches at El Tajín Ea 8125
Cat.No.39

30 Photograph of the Pyramid of the Niches at El Tajín, May 1989

31 Front view of the Pyramid of the Niches at El Tajín Ea 8144, Cat.No.40

32 Front view of a female Jalisco figure from the Mound of Guadalupe Ea 8251a, Cat.No.41

33 Side view of a female Jalisco figure from the Mound of Guadalupe Ea 8251c, Cat.No.42

34 Front view of male ceramic figure from the Mound of Guadalupe Ea 8251e, Cat.No.43

35 (*above*) View of the courtyard of the Palace of the Columns at Mitla Ea 8279, Cat.No.45
36 (*below*) View of the courtyard of the Palace of the Columns at Mitla, May 1989

37 View through a doorway of the ruins at Mitla Ea 8277, Cat.No.46

38 View of the west façade of the Pyramid of the Magician at Uxmal Ea 8123, Cat.No.47

39 View of the Nunnery Quadrangle at Uxmal Ea 8224, Cat.No.48

40 Sketch of the east wall of the Temple of the Feathered Serpent at Xochicalco Ea 8273b, Cat.No.49

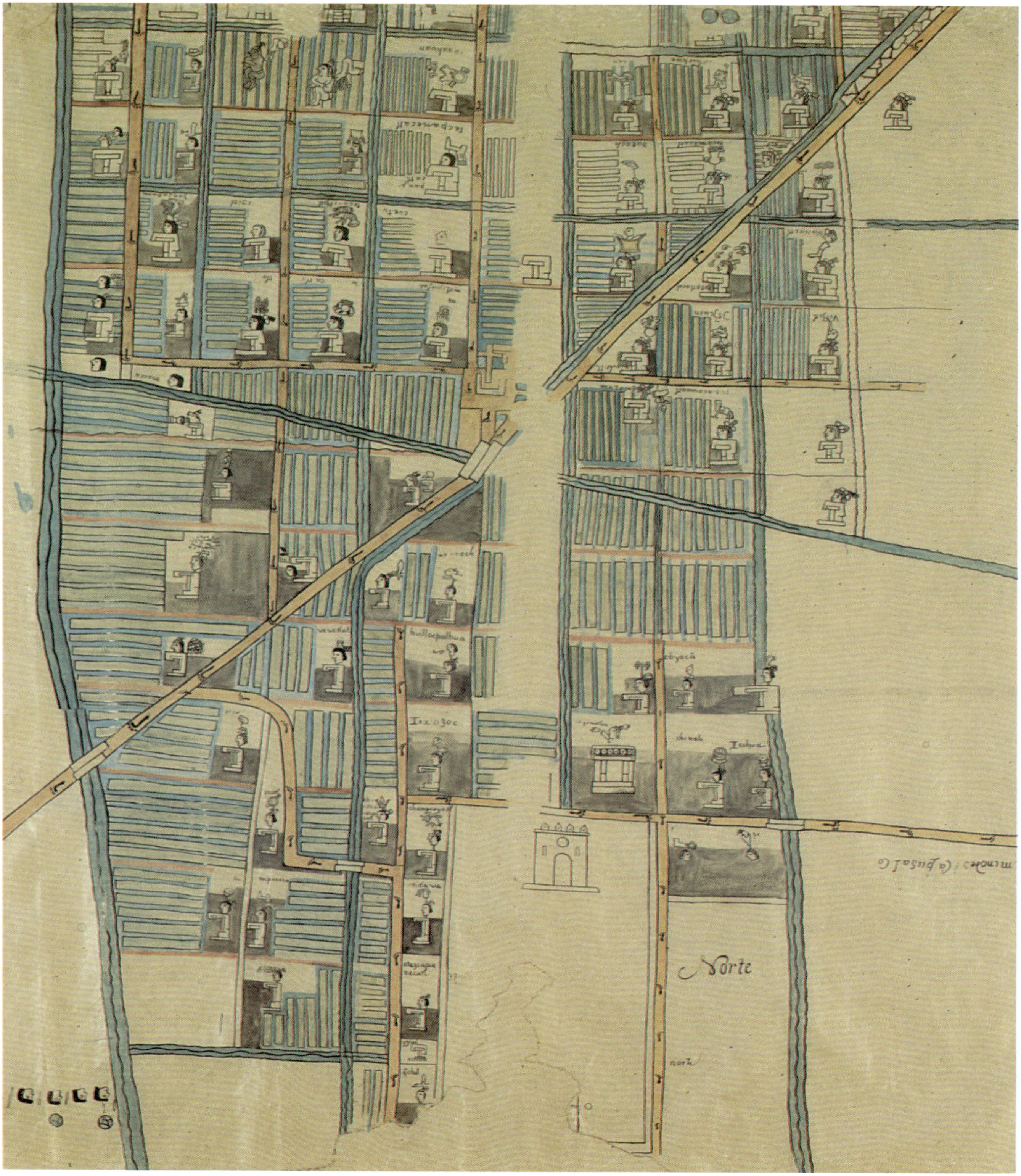

41 Copy of part of the Maguey Plan Ea 8367a, Cat.No.50

42 View of the remains of the Great Pyramid at Cholula with the Church of Nuestra Señora de los Remedios built on top. Ea 8145, Cat.No.51

43 Sketch of old house in San Andres Chalchicomula Ea 8403, Cat.No.54

44 Sketch of the town of San Andres Chalchicomula Ea 8401, Cat.No.55

45 Sketch of the cathedral at Aguascalientes Ea 8148, Cat.No.57

46 Sketch of view of Tlaxcala Ea 8406, Cat.No.62

47 (*above*) Sketch of an unknown market place Ea 8422, Cat.No.65
48 (*below*) Page of a sketchbook, showing a distant view of Guadalajara and Barranca (gorge), dated 2.97 Ea 9493 – *not in exhibition*

49 Page of sketchbook, showing a view of the thatched wooden houses of Naranjo, on the road to Campo Morado, dated 9.2.98. At the bottom of the page, a pencil sketch of a 'cocoon of caterpillar with sharp black claws'. Ea 9493 – *not in exhibition*

50 Page of sketchbook, showing a watercolour sketch of a Totonac girl, Papantla, dated 2.12.94. The girl wears the traditional red embroidered skirt of Totonac Indian women, which has today been replaced by white lace. Ea 8374 – *not in exhibition*

The Objects

Very little of Adela Breton's collection came from proper excavations and so dates and cultures are assigned on stylistic grounds. Most of the objects are from Western Mexico, Pablo Solorio's home area: identification here is made more difficult by a lack of controlled excavation in the area, so that comparisons cannot be made with provenanced, dated material. Most of the dates and cultures given here are, therefore, tentative.

66 Tripod vessel
Churumuco, Michoacan State
?Late Classic (?Chapala)

Pottery tripod vessel with applied animal head (?coyote) and mould made feet in shape of a bearded human head, with burnished surface and line and dot decoration. The feet are from the same mould as those on E 5875. Perhaps Chapala Ware. H.169 mm
Ea 8102

67 Tripod bowl
Churumuco, Michoacan State
?Late Classic (?Chapala)

Pottery tripod bowl, the interior and exterior wall burnished, underside and legs unburnished. Mould-made feet in the form of a bearded human head, from the same mould as Ea 08102. Dia.258 mm
E 5875

68 Tripod bowl
Michoacan State
?Late Classic (?Chapala)

Shallow clay tripod bowl with hand-built hollow feet in the shape of an animal head, (?deer); burnished red surface with band of white painted scroll decoration and white slip on animal heads. Perhaps Chapala Ware. Dia.188 mm
Ea 8101

27 *Two tripod vessels, probably Chapala ware, with legs cast from the same mould, see Cat.Nos. 66-67*

28 *Pottery bowls and vessels, see Cat.Nos. (L to R) 68, 69, 73, 71*

69 Tripod bowl
Churumuco, Michoacan State
?Pre-Classic

Shallow clay bowl on 3 plain legs, with carinated shoulder. Burnished red ware, probably with a moulded base and hand-raised rim. Possibly Río Balsas type pottery. Dia.28 mm
E 5876

70 Leg of tripod bowl?
Nuhualac, Mexico State
Post-Classic (Aztec)

Hollow pottery, mould-made head attached to hand-built body, hole in underside of head and in body near head. [Called a flute by AB, but probably the leg of a large tripod vessel, or possibly a handle for an ?incense burner.] L.143 mm
E 4916

71 Trefoil vase
Nochistlan, Zacatecas State
?Early Classic (?W. Mexico)

Pottery vase with three-lobed body and narrow neck; cream slip with red and ochre outlines; burnished. The style is West Mexican (Nayarit or Jalisco perhaps) rather than Zacatecan. H.114 mm
E 5059

72 Vessel
Chapala, Jalisco State
?Late Pre-Classic (?Nayarit)

Round-bottomed clay pot, with a cross painted on the surface in red. Dia.104 mm
Ea 8120

73 Vessel
Churumuco, Michoacan State
?Late Pre-Classic

Round-bodied clay vessel, with upper half slipped and burnished a darker red with two black lines as decoration: perhaps Chupicuaro Ware. Dia.110 mm
E 5061

74 Bowl
Ozumba, Mexico State
?Pre-Classic

Clay bowl in the shape of a lying dog; tail, one leg and one ear broken. Clay pellets form the nose and eyes. [Vessels in the shape of dogs are common from the Colima area of Western Mexico, but this particular bowl is not in Colima style.] H.79 mm
E 5066

75 Vase
Ozumba, Mexico State
Pre-Classic (?Colima)

Small clay vase, straight sided, with applied human head and limbs of rolled clay; one hand holding rim of vase and legs folded under body. The head looking upwards, with a hair crest or headdress and large hole in earlobe. Probably Colima Ware. Dia.58 mm
E 5065

76 Tripod bowl
Mexico D.F.
?Post-Classic (?Aztec)

Shallow pottery tripod bowl, with four black lines decorating the inner rim. Feet broken and missing. Dia.152 mm
Ea 8467

77 Mortar/*molcajete*
Casa Zinzen, Coyoacan, Mexico D.F.
Post-Classic (Aztec)

Part of red pottery mortar, a shallow dish on three legs with incised roughened base for grinding chilli and other foods.
Ea 10635

78 Bowl
Ozumba, Mexico State
undated

Pottery bowl, with burnished surface abraded on upper half. Dia.182 mm
E 5069

79 Jug
Ozumba, Mexico State
undated

Small pottery jug, probably plain domestic ware. H.145 mm
E 5062

80 Tripod bowl
Churumuco, Michoacan State
?Post-Classic (Tarascan)

Miniature tripod vessel, restored, with burnished red inner surface and incised and painted ?snail design on the flat rim. [Miniature pots were placed in burials. This type of bowl has been described as used for spinning; it is still quite common for hand-spinners to place the end of the spindle in a bowl, giving a smooth clean surface and controlling the spindle's movement.] Dia.49 mm
E 5046

81 Whistle
Tzintzúntzan, Michoacan State
?Post-Classic (?Tarascan)

Pottery whistle in the shape of a flying bird. The crest on the head suggests a macaw or similar bird. Buff coloured and ?hand-made. L.40 mm
E 4917

82 Whistle
Tzintzúntzan, Michoacan State
?Post-Classic (?Tarascan)

Pottery whistle in the shape of a sitting bird, with a broken mouthpiece. Probably mould-made, with a slipped and burnished finish and traces of white in tail and wing detail. L.43 mm
E 4918

83 Incense burner
Churumuco, Michoacan State
?Post-Classic (?Toltec or ?Tarascan)

Large pottery vessel. Described by AB as a funerary urn. Large hourglass-shaped vessel, with deep foot ring, two slashed bands at top and bottom of three and four rows of nodules, the foot ring with two holes pierced through: interior slightly blackened, perhaps from use as burner. [These are very similar to the pottery incense burners found in a Toltec offering in the Cave of Balankanche in Yucatán: Toltec trade and influence was widespread, although these could be locally made Tarascan products.]Dia.269 mm
E 5072

84 Incense burner
Churumuco, Michoacan State
?Post-Classic (?Toltec or ?Tarascan)

Described by AB as a funerary urn. Large hourglass-shaped vessel, with deep foot ring, decorated with 4 slashed bands and 2 rows of nodules at top and 1 row of nodules at bottom: interior blackened, perhaps from use as burner, with traces of white on exterior. Dia.250 mm
E 5073

85 *Candelero*
Mexico
?Early Classic (?Teotihuacán)

Pottery two-holed *candelero* with thumb-impressed decoration. [*Candelero* or candlestick describes the shape, though the function of these objects is not known - one theory is that they were used to hold the blood offered to the gods as a self-sacrifice, another that they were incense burners.] H.53 mm
E 5922

29 Incense burner, used for burning copal as an offering to the gods, see Cat.No. 84

86 Five vessels
Chapala, Jalisco State
?Early Post-Classic

Five miniature pottery vessels with pierced lugs: probably votive offerings. [Miniature votive vases have been found at lakeside sites around Lake Chapala.] H.14-30 mm
E 5052-6

87 Two incense burners
Chapala, Jalisco State
?Early Post-Classic

Two miniature incense burners, in the shape of a round-bowled spoon with claw finial, with ?pigment in bowls. [The claw finial could represent a turkey claw, symbol of the god Tezcatlipoca.] L.88 mm and 87 mm
E 5057-8

88 Pipe
Tzintzúntzan, Michoacan State
?Post-Classic (?Toltec)

Tobacco pipe with flared bowl and stem decorated with undulating serpent frills. L.115 mm
E 4973

89 Figurine
Mezcala, Guerrero State
?Late Pre-Classic (Mezcala)

Carved stone human figurine in abstract style. [These figures are known from looted sites and thus are difficult to date. The only scientifically excavated ones come from Aztec offerings in the Great Temple in Mexico City, suggesting that the Mezcala tradition continued to at least the 14th century AD, or that the Aztecs themselves reused looted pieces.] H.120 mm
E 5107

90 Figurine
Mezcala, Guerrero State
?Late Pre-Classic (Mezcala)

Carved stone human figure in abstract style. H.130 mm
E 5109

91 Figurine
Ozumba, Mexico State
Pre-Classic

Clay figurine of ?male figure, wearing a loincloth and headdress, with necklace, earstuds, sandals and bracelets in applied strips of clay. H.87 mm
E 4948

92 Head of figurine
Metepec, Mexico State
?Pre-Classic

Head of female figurine, with applied clay features and braided hair and red pigment on neck. H.34 mm
Ea 10828

93 Head of figurine
Apizco
?Pre-Classic

Pottery head of a ?female figurine, with applied clay features and turban. H.49 mm
Ea 10067

30 Miniature pottery vessels and incense burners, probably votice offerings from Lake Chapala, see Cat.Nos. 86-87

31 Pottery figurines, see Cat.Nos. (top, L to R) 94, 100, 109, 99, (bottom, L to R) 105, 104, 91

94 Figurine
Chapala, Jalisco State
?Proto-Classic (Nayarit)

Female figurine, in 'Chinesca' style, with stylised features, high square forehead. wing-like ears, pointed chin, slashed eyes and mouth and very large nose: the legs broken off. H.211 mm
E 5087

95 Head of figure
Chapala, Jalisco State
?Proto-Classic (Nayarit)

Pottery head of a figure, with sloping square forehead, large holes through ears, long nose and slashed eyes and mouth. Red ?slip on face except across eyes and cheeks and upper lip. Black traces over the red may be tar or pitch. H.76 mm
E 4929

96 Head of figure
[Ixtlan] del Rio, Nayarit State
?Pre-Classic or Early Classic (Nayarit)

Hollow pottery head of Nayarit figure, with red slip on face, white eyes, multiple earrings and multiple noserings, red (plait of hair?) and white twisted band around head.
H.195 mm
E 5086

97 Head of figure
Ozumba, Mexico State
undated

Hollow clay head broken from a figure: ?male, wearing earstuds and a head band with disc attached at front; with prominent mouth and teeth, applied pellet eyes, and red and yellow pigment. Possibly a type of Southern Jalisco pottery. H.112 mm
E 4942

98 Head of figurine
Texcoco, Mexico State
Early Classic (Teotihuacán III and IV)

Pottery head from a dancing figure, in typical Teotihuacán style.
H.35 mm
Ea 10480

99 Figurine
Teotihuacán, Mexico State
?Late Classic (?Teotihuacán IV or V)

Small clay figurine of seated ?man, wearing tunic or cape and cloak tied in front of neck, with earstuds and headress. Mould made, with plain back. H.59 mm
E 4925

100 Figure
Cleapata?, Jalisco State
Early Classic (Zacatecas)

Hollow pottery figure of woman, very flat, with painted or tattooed patterns on body in red and black. Hands on hips, lower part of body lost. H.167 mm
Ea 8458

101 'Smiling Face' figurine
Mound of El Pantano, Oaxaca State/border Veracruz State
Late Classic (Remojadas II)

Hollow pottery head of 'Smiling Face' figurine, with headdress and earstuds. [These infantile figures were mass produced, using clay moulds for parts like the face, and hand modelling to join the parts together. It is suggested that these smiling faces represent the result of an ecstatic ritual (M.Miller 1986)] H.138 mm
E 5088

102 Head of figurine
San Pedro, Oaxaca State
?Late Classic (Zapotec)

Pottery head from mould-made figurine, with elaborate headdress and earstuds. Headdress has the typical owl head on the right side and feathers on the left. H.109 mm
E 5084

103 Mould
S.Francisco, Mexico D.F.
?Late Classic

Pottery mould for head and torso of figure with separate limbs. H.57 mm
Ea 10483

104 Figurine
Tula, Hidalgo State
Post-Classic (Toltec)

Small pottery figurine of a ?female, wearing ornate headdress. Mould-made, with plain back. H.87 mm
E 4924

105 Figurine
Teotaltiche, Jalisco State
Post-Classic (Toltec)

Small pottery figurine of a female, wearing elaborate headdress. Mould-made, with plain back: legs broken and missing: traces of blue pigment on body. H.49 mm
E 4923

32 Heads from pottery figurines, see Cat.Nos. (top, L to R) 101, 95 (bottom, L to R) 95, 102, 97

106 Mould
Tzintzúntzan, Michoacan State
undated - ?Post-Classic (?Tarascan)

Pottery mould for ape-like figure: hands on knees, pot belly, open mouth, prognathous, with long hair and collar or necklace. H.61 mm
E 5075

107 Heads of figurines
Otumba, Mexico State
Late Post-Classic and Colonial (Aztec and Colonial)

24 heads of pottery figurines, mould-made, showing different degrees of detail. All show a face with headdress, some plain, some ornate. [All are Aztec in style; production of local goods continued after the Spanish Conquest.] H.17-60 mm
Ea 10194

108 Figurine
Ozumba, Mexico State
Late Post-Classic or Early Colonial (Aztec or Colonial)

Pottery figurine, now broken and incomplete, of a baby in a chair with bar across the front - like a high chair. [This is probably a rare representation of a child sacrifice: in early spring, at the ritual of Altcoualo, districts and villages chose a child for sacrifice, and it was carried in a decorated chair to a river and drowned. The sacrifice and the accompanying crying was for the rain gods, so that they would send rain.] H.60 mm
Ea 10915

109 Figure
Churumuco, Michoacan State
undated

Pottery female figure, arms broken at shoulder, with square head and protruding features, the applied headdress broken off forehead. H.104 mm
E 5083

110 Head of figurine
Tula, Hidalgo State
undated ?late period

Pottery head of figurine, with very square head, hair framing face, with applied clay features. H.29 mm
Ea 10521

111 Adzehead
Xochipala, Guerrero State
undated

Stone adze-head, partly polished: rectangular in section with a flat butt. [Metal tools were relatively rare after the introduction of metallurgy to Mexico in about AD 900, and stone tools remained important.] L.95 mm
E 4964

112 Missile point/knife blade
Churumuco, Michoacan State
?Post-Classic

Leaf-shaped blade of a type called a Lerma point, bifacially worked. L.144 mm
E 4989

113 Missile point/knife blade
Churumuco, Michoacan State
?Post-Classic

A stone blade of the type called an ?Angostura point, bifacially worked. [A similar style blade was found in the Sacred Cenote at Chichén Itzá, hafted to a wooden handle, and described as a sacrificial knife. Coggins 1984: no.26.] L.155 mm
E 4990

114 Rubber or polisher
Tzintzúntzan, Michoacan State
?Post-Classic (?Tarascan)

Rectangular rubber or polisher of lava, with handle cut in one piece with rubber. [Information with the object said that it was used for rubbing down plaster stucco before painting it.] L.73 mm
Ea 8472

115 Rubber
Zacoalco
undated

Stone rubber, polished with use. L.107 mm
Ea 10583

116 Core
Island, Lake of Magdalena, Jalisco State
undated

Large obsidian or volcanic glass core, showing scars where blades have been struck. [Adela Breton was particularly interested in worked obsidian, and collected many cores and blades from the main factory sites. (Breton 1902).] L.124 mm
E 5021

117 Core
Mitla, Oaxaca State
undated

Small obsidian core, from which flakes or blades have been struck. L.48 mm
Ea 10810

118 Three flakes/blades
Teuchitlan, Jalisco State
undated

Obsidian or volcanic glass flakes. L.103-181 mm
E 5023-4, 5026

119 Four flakes/blades
Ixtaccihuatl, Nahualac, Mexico State
undated

Four obsidian flakes or blades. L.43-81 mm
Ea 10816

120 Macehead
Chapala, Jalisco State
undated

Marble macehead, ball shaped with 5 projections. D.83 mm
E 4981

121 *Atlatl* finger grip
Churumuco, Michoacan State
?Postclassic

Steatite finger grip for atlatl or spear thrower, an asymmetrical loop with incised grooves and 2 holes for attachment to atlatl. [Finger grips were tied to the lower third of the atlatl shaft when there was no integral finger hole. Use of a spear thrower increased the range and power of a throw.] W.35 mm
E 5112

122 *Atlatl* finger grip
Churumuco, Michoacan State
?Post-Classic

Jadeite finger grip for atlatl or spear thrower, a shallow loop with a bar across the top, the bar with a stylised head at each end with one eye drilled for ?inlay and two holes for attachment. W.35 mm
E 5113

123 *Atlatl* finger grip
Zacapicharo
?Post-Classic

Shell finger grip for an atlatl or spear thrower, asymmetrical loop with raised rim and two holes for attachment. W.43 mm
E 5114

124 Arrow or dart head
Zacapicharo
undated

Obsidian barbed and tanged arrowhead, with one barb broken, bifacially worked. [The bow and arrow had limited distribution in Mexico, being mainly used by the barbarian *Chichemeca*. Darts thrown using the atlatl or spear thrower had similar heads.] L.47 mm
Ea 11745

125 Necklace
Churumuco, Michoacan State
undated

Necklace of tubular beads and shell discs, the tubes formed by marine worms. Restrung. L.68 mm
E 4900

126 Necklace
Churumuco, Michoacan State
undated

Necklace of shell beads, with small ring beads, triangular pendants, square plaques with large central hole, long shell pendant, tube bead and jade ring bead and pendant. Restrung. L.52 mm
E 4899

127 Beads
Churumuco, Michoacan State
undated

Necklace of shell beads, three large ones with spiral of shell, and 17 worked ball beads. [Note from AB - used as currency?] L.345 mm
E 4959

128 Frog beads
Churumuco, Michoacan State
?Post-Classic (?Tarascan)

Five shell beads carved in likeness of frogs, with two holes at side for suspension or attachment. Two different types of bead: three smaller with protruding front legs, two larger more stylised and compact. L.31-38 mm
E 4898

129 Bead/pendant
Zacapicharo
undated

Shell bead, pink, with two holes for suspension, possibly cut down from larger bead (from the remains of two holes on top edge). L.26 mm
Ea 10473

130 Plaque
Churumuco, Michoacan State
?Post-Classic (?Tarascan)

Jade plaque with two angled perforations, showing a human head emerging from the jaws of a bird or animal. W.73 mm
E 4910

131 Pendant
Nopales, [?Nogales, Veracruz State or ?Nopala, Hidalgo State]
undated

Jade pendant or amulet in the shape of a bird. L.50 mm
E 4908

132 Discs/earstuds
Ozumba, Mexico State
undated

Pottery discs with slightly concave sides; earstuds or lip plugs, perhaps of Chupiaro Ware. [Earstuds and lip plugs were a common adornment: in style they ranged from plain ceramic to highly decorated precious metals or carved jade]. Dia.19-30 mm
E 4963

133 Earstuds
Ozumba, Mexico State
undated

Pottery discs with slightly concave sides, earstuds or lip plugs, perhaps of Chupiaro Ware. Dia.13-28 mm
Ea 10834

134 Paint stamp
Tenayuca
?Post-Classic (?Aztec)

Pottery stamp mould-made with figure of a monkey, a common design. [Stamps were used to decorate the face or body, using a natural dye like red cochineal.] H.64 mm
E 5080

135 Stamp
Huexotla
?Post-Classic (?Aztec)

Pottery stamp with design of glyphs, used to decorate the face or body. Mould made, now broken at both ends. One glyph is that for feast, *Ilhuitl.* L.38 mm
Ea 9976

136 Pear-shaped bell
Churumuco, Michoacan State
?Post-Classic

Pear shaped copper bell, with decoration on platform and shoulder: cast by the lost wax process, with pellet missing. [Metallurgy was introduced late into Mexico and this could be an import from Central America rather than locally made.] L.101 mm
E 5091

137 Five spherical bells
Churumuco, Michoacan State
?Post-Classic

Five spherical copper bells with decoration on one side. Cast by the lost wax process, each with small metal pellet. [Metallurgy was introduced late into Mexico, from the Andean area of South America. Most of the metalwork was ornamental, like the very common small bells.] Dia.15 mm
E 5093-4, 5096-8

138 Mortar
Churumuco, Michoacan State
?Post-Classic (Tarascan)

Stone mortar in form of a ?leather-back turtle, with on one side a smooth grinding surface, with outlined rim, and raised decoration on the back consisting of a central ridge and three concentric rings of raised dots, with a head and tail. Dia.139 mm
Ea 8106

139 Jalisco figure
Mound of Guadalupe, Etzatlán, Jalisco State
?Late Pre-Classic or Early Classic (Jalisco)

Standing female figure of hollow pottery: stylised figure with thick-set body and high forehead, holding a bowl to her left shoulder. Surface decoration of burnished slip, with body painting or tattooing on face, breasts and stomach, and painted skirt: applied clay bangles, multiple earrings and nosering. Jalisco figure of 'El Arenal Brown' type, a type so far found only in the burials of the Magdalena Lake area. Part of a grave group. H.446 mm
Ea 8100

140 Figure
Mound of Guadalupe, Etzatlán, Jalisco State
?Late Pre-Classic or Early Classic (?Jalisco)

Standing female figure of hollow pottery: stylised figure with stocky body, short arms and thick legs, with narrow forehead and scarification on shoulders. Traces of painted surface remain, perhaps like Ea 8100 with painted clothing and body decoration. Part of a grave group. H.39 mm
E 5103

141 Bowl
Mound of Guadalupe, Etzatlán, Jalisco State
?Late Pre-Classic or Early Classic (?Nayarit)

Clay bowl with narrow mouth and carinated shoulder in buff clay with red painted decoration: chequerboard pattern on shoulder and concentric rings around rim, inside and out, and a yellow hatched design on the base. Part of a grave group. Dia.180 mm
E 5067

142 Armlet
Mound of Guadalupe, Etzatlán, Jalisco State
?Late Pre-Classic or Early Classic

Shell armlet cut from a marine shell, undecorated. Part of a grave group. Dia.112 mm
E 5194

143 Bracelet/armlet
Mound of Guadalupe, Etzatlán, Jalisco State
?Late Pre-Classic or Early Classic

Shell armlet cut from a marine shell, with carved decoration of frogs. Part of a grave group. Dia.107 mm
E 5913

144 Bracelet/armlet
Mound of Guadalupe, Etzatlán, Jalisco State
?Late Pre-Classic or Early Classic

Narrow shell armlet cut from marine shell (probably *Glycymeris gigantea*) with carved decoration in form of double-headed serpents with triangular heads and zigzag bodies, with frogs between the serpents. Part of grave group. Dia.84 mm
E 4907

145 Beads
Mound of Guadalupe, Etzatlán, Jalisco State
?Late Pre-Classic or Early Classic

Necklace of shell and coral beads and pendants. 3 long tubular beads of ?coral, 6 stylised bird shaped shell beads, 4 rectangular beads with a ?frog incised on top and 3 ?coral pendant figures, 1 of them a stylised ?human. Restrung. Part of a grave group. L.235 mm
Ea 8462

146 Implement?
Mound of Guadalupe, Etzatlán, Jalisco State
?Late Pre-Classic or Early Classic

Prism-shaped stone ?implement of unknown use. Part of a grave group. L.75 mm
Ea 9967

147 Core
Mound of Guadalupe, Etzatlán, Jalisco State
?Late Pre-Classic or Early Classic

Obsidian core, showing parallel scars where blades have been removed for use as tools. Part of a grave group. L.149 mm
Ea 10410

148 Flake
Mound of Guadalupe, Etzatlán, Jalisco State
?Late Pre-Classic or Early Classic

Obsidian flake. Part of a grave group. L.69 mm
Ea 9968

149 Doorway
Upper Temple of the Jaguars, Chichén Itzá, Yucatán State
Post-Classic (Toltec-Maya)

Reconstruction of the Inner Doorway of the Upper Temple of the Jaguars, situated between the Outer and Inner Chambers: plaster casts made from Maudslay's casts. On the door jambs are Toltec warrior figures: K4, Rodent, and K9, Snake, face the Inner Chamber. Two lintels above the door, one carved and the other plain; on the carved lintel, Captain Sun Disc and Captain Serpent face each other, a mask with waterlilies between them, and the head of a bicephalic serpent at each end. H. to lintel 2616 mm
Ea 8427-9, 8432-6

150 Silver disc
Churumco, Michoacan State
?Post-Classic

Disc of thin sheet metal, with punched line decoration: probably part of an earing, with remains of hole for attachment in broken edge. [although not an outstandingly beautiful object, this disc is important as the only piece of pre-Hispanic Mexican silverwork in Britain] Dia. 60 mm
E4895

A Very Brief History Of Mexico

The human history of Mexico stretches back to about 25,000 BC, but knowledge of the pre-Hispanic period comes from limited sources: a few 'painted books' or codices, inscriptions, Spanish writings on their new colony and archaeological finds. The following account is therefore subject to change as work on the sources reinterprets what is known.

Human occupation is known from about 25,000 BC, when semi-nomadic groups lived by gathering and hunting, using stone tools.

Archaeologists divide the early history into four periods: the Archaic, Pre-Classic or Formative, Classic or Florescent and Post-Classic, according to the degree of development.

In the **Archaic** period, c. 6500 - 2000 BC, there is evidence of settled habitation with the small-scale cultivation of maize and other vegetable foods, though gathering and hunting was still important for food.

In the **Pre-Classic** period c. 1500 BC - AD 150, the basic Meso-American pattern was established, with the emergence of a governing élite and an organised priesthood (represented archaeologically by palaces and temples) and also specialised craftsmen and artists. The mass of the population consisted of peasant farmers living in villages around the centre and available for work, to build and maintain the city and to supply food to its inhabitants.

The first of the great Mexican civilisations developed in the Gulf area; the **Olmec** people established cities like La Venta and began the development of a calendar, hieroglyphic writing system and a pantheon of gods which were spread throughout Mexico and used by all later Meso-American cultures. In Central Mexico, **Monte Albán** was the great centre of the **Zapotec** people in Oaxaca, begun in the Middle Pre-Classic and abandoned at the end of the Classic period.

During the **Classic** period, c. AD 150 - 900, **Teotihuacán** became the dominant centre. Nothing is known of the people behind the Teotihuacán civilisation, although they built a city which covered over nine square miles, laid out on a grid plan, with ceremonial, administrative and residential buildings; at its height an estimated 200,000 people lived there. The influence of Teotihuacán was widespread, yet like the great Olmec centres, Teotihuacán was deliberately destroyed for unknown political, economic or enviromental reasons, in about 750 AD.

Xochicalco became important with the decline of Teotihuacán in the late Classic. Its architecture suggests heavy influence from the Maya and contact with cultures all over Mexico. **El Tajín**, perhaps built by the Totonac people, was the most important Veracruz site. In the **Maya** region (the Yucatán peninsula and Chiapas in Mexico, and the states of Guatemala, Belize and Honduras), the Classic period saw the greatest achievements in art, architecture and scientific study; the major centres here like

Palenqué, **Uxmal** and **Chichén** saw much building, but they also declined and were abandoned, although in the Yucatán new ideas and perhaps invasion from central Mexico brought a revival (Fig. 33).

There was a general decline throughout Mexico and the Maya area: the collapse of Teotihuacán would have affected trade throughout the whole country, but why did the city decline? Theories include ecological disaster, agricultural failure or attack by the **Toltec** people. Whatever the cause, the unifying force in the area was removed and the great city-states were replaced by petty kingdoms.

The **Post-Classic** period, c. AD 900 - 1520, in the wake of this collapse, saw a number of invasions by 'barbarian' tribes, each briefly in the ascendancy. A characteristic of the Post-Classic was a greater emphasis on militarism, with professional warriors now at the top of the social hierarchy rather than religious or political leaders. The **Chichimeca** 'barbarians' were semi-nomadic peoples from the desert areas of the north, where agriculture was impossible. The **Toltec** were one such *Chichimeca* group, who controlled the central area from about AD 950 to 1150, taking most of their ideas from Teotihuacán. They were a very militaristic people, with war providing captives for sacrifice to the gods. The great city of **Tula** was deserted in the twelfth century, after drought and internal conflict, and the Toltec were dispersed throughout Mexico. The city was destroyed, probably by another group of *Chichimeca* (Fig. 34).

There were other important states in this period. A new **Zapotec** centre was established at **Mitla**, after Monte Albán was abandoned at the end of the Classic period. Mitla was still inhabited when the Spanish arrived. By about AD 1350, the **Mixtec** people from the Mixteca area of Oaxaca began to infiltrate the Zapotec area, by both warfare and judicious marriages: within two hundred years they had taken over almost all of the Zapotec sites. The **Tarascan** people were another *Chichimeca* group who moved into Michoacán and established their own culture with their capital at **Tzintzúntzan**. Great artists and architects, they withstood the Aztec, and remained an independent kingdom to the Spanish Conquest.

33 (left) Pen and ink sketch of the ruins at Labna, Yucatán State, 9.4.1901. From a sketchbook. Ea 9494

34 (right) Pen and ink drawing of the serpent-headed sandal of a statue leg at Tula, the Toltec capital. Ea 9496

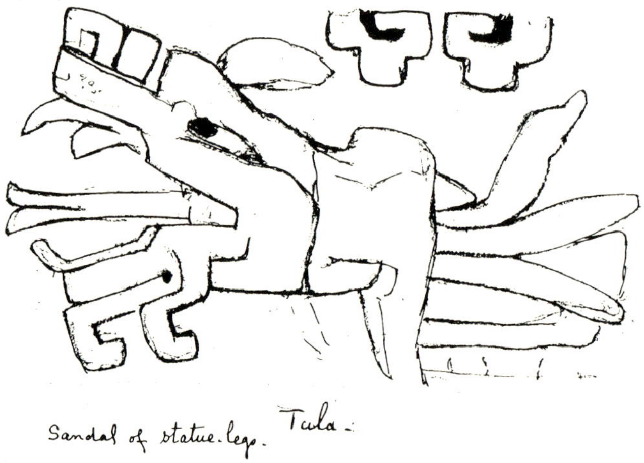

After the fall of Tula and the collapse of the Toltec empire, there was anarchy in central Mexico, with *Chichimeca* establishing small city-states. The **Aztec** or **Mexica** were the last of the *Chichimeca* who moved into central Mexico in about AD 1200, a time when no one city-state was dominant. The Aztec worked as labourers or mercenaries, but their bloodthirsty habits made them unendearing as neighbours. In 1345 they settled on an island in a lake, founding the city of **Tenochtitlan** which became the capital of the Aztec empire and the Mexico City of today. They served as mercenaries for the strongest of the city-states and helped to overcome the others. In 1427, the Aztecs also overcame their ally and took over the expanding state, eventually controlling most of central and southern Mexico. They also rewrote history, with themselves as the heirs to the Toltecs.

In the **Maya** area, during the Post-Classic period, Mexican influence appeared in the Yucatán. **Chichén Itzá** revived (after a general Maya decline in about AD 900) and became the centre of the state, controlled perhaps by the Toltec from central Mexico, perhaps by the Putun, a mexicanised Maya group. Later, the site came under the control of another mexicanised group, the Itzá. They flourished briefly, and then Chichén Itzá was abandoned and left to squatters. The Maya were never conquered by the Aztec, but after the fifteenth century there was no great centre of authority, as Chichén Itzá, then **Mayapán** had been, only small independent city states.

The **Spanish Conquest** of Mexico began when Hernán Cortés and 550 men landed near Cempoala on 21 April 1519. This small force was able to defeat the Aztec war machine because of superior weapons, the willingness of disaffected Indian groups to ally with Cortés against the Aztecs and the Aztec leader Motecuhzoma's belief that Cortés was the god Quetzalcoatl, which prevented him from acting decisively against the Spaniard. In 1521, after a long siege, Tenochtitlan fell to the Spanish and Mexico became a colony of Spain. The Yucatán and the Maya proved harder to conquer: the colonial capital of Mérida was not established until 1542.

By the end of the century 'New Spain' stretched from Panama to the western states of North America. The Indian population was profoundly affected by the conquest: in 1521 there were about 25 million Indians and by 1800 only 3 million. The majority had died of new illnesses, like influenza, brought by the Spanish and the remainder were virtually enslaved as landless labourers, with few if any rights. The colonial power brought Christianity to the people, and took gold, silver and other products back to Spain.

Independence from Spain came slowly. Spanish dominance of Mexico's trade and government was resented by the Mexican Spanish population, with the first open rebellions in 1810 and 1813.

The armies of these revolutions were composed of Indians and *Mestizos*, who had little or no power or influence in political affairs. In 1820 the *Creole* population which held land, wealth and positions of power in the army and state, joined the rebels, and with this backing Mexico became independent of Spain in 1821. The new **Republic** still had many problems to overcome and went through many changes of government.

In 1836 **Texas**, then part of Mexico, declared independence; in 1838 France invaded Veracruz and in 1845 Mexico and the U.S.A. went to war, resulting in the permanent loss of Texas, New Mexico and California to the U.S.

In 1855 a **reform movement** began, to limit the power of the immensely rich church. This polarised liberal and conservative groups and brought, by request, French intervention and a puppet French emperor, who was overthrown in 1867.

The dictatorship of **Porfirio Diaz**, from 1877, saw a policy of modernisation, as railways, roads, industry and telegraph systems transformed Mexico.

Modernisation was financed by foreign investors: resentment of this and lack of opportunity under a dictatorship produced a middle-class opposition, joined by the landless debt-ridden Indian peasants.

In 1910 **revolution** began, led by **Francisco Madero** and supported by guerrilla groups led by men like **Pancho Villa** and **Emilio Zapata**. Although the revolution succeeded in overthrowing the dictatorship, fighting continued over policy and leadership. It was not until 1924 that the **Revolutionary Constitution** was put into effect; public works began on roads and irrigation systems, land was redistributed to villages as communal holdings and education was improved.

In 1934 the **Party of the Institutionalised Revolution** (PRI), was elected to power, and has retained power at every election since.

PRI policy continues to modernise and advance the country. Mexico today has heavy foreign debts, made worse by falling oil revenues which financed expansion in the 1960s; the austerity forced on the country to repay those debts has helped to fuel the problems of unemployment, aided by a massive population increase.

Although Mexico is the most stable nation in Latin America, it is to an extent polarised: northern Mexico is heavily influenced by the U.S., and by conservative business interests; in the more rural south, radical influences are dominant, with land redistribution still a major demand.

Tourism is now a major industry and earner of foreign currency; visitors are attracted by the climate, the surfing, and by the archaeological remains of the past great civilisations. Which brings us back to the Olmec...

Sue Giles

Glossary

'Wail of the deer'.	**Acancéh**
Atlantes, male figures used architecturally as supporting columns.	**Atlantean**
A spear or dart thrower, used to give more power and distance to a throw.	***Atlatl***
'The people whose face no one knows'. They called themselves the *Mexica.*	***Aztecs***
In Maya mythology, these were the four gods who held up the skies above a flat earth.	**Bacab**
Playing ground for the ball game: courts varied in shape and size in different areas and periods, but a common style was I shaped, with straight or sloping sides and a ring set in the side wall. Important sites had several courts. See also *Tlachtli.*	**Ball court**
The island Arawak word for a local leader. The term was spread from the Caribbean by the Spanish and was widely adopted in Colonial Meso-America.	***Cacique***
Pertaining to a calendar. (See also Maya Long Count).	**Calendric**
Strictly, a female figure used architecturally as a supporting column : used by Adela Breton to describe the stone standing figures who held up a stone table top.	**Caryatid**
A natural well, formed by the collapse of the limestone roof of an underground water source.	***Cenote***
Central area of the Maya realm, which included part of Campeche in Mexico, Belize and parts of Guatemala. In this area the Maya culture reached its peak during the Classic period.	**Central Maya**
Rain god, also known to the Aztecs as Tlaloc, depicted as a masked figure.	**Chac**
A variant of the central Yucatán architectural style.	**Chenes**
'Lineage of the dog', a general name given to the 'barbarian' invaders from northern Mexico. The Aztec were the most famous *Chichimeca* tribe.	***Chichimeca***
'The mouth of the well of the Itzá'.	**Chichén Itzá**
'Floating gardens'; the Aztec settled on an island in a shallow lake and built islands to extend the city and to give land on which to grow food.	***Chinampas***
A Mayan language still spoken within a small area of Mexico.	***Chol (Cholti)***
A manuscript or 'painted book', drawn on folded deerskin or bark paper. The books covered religious matters and ceremony, history, astronomy, royal genealogies and social ritual. Pictoral works, with any names or texts written in glyphs, they were meant to be interpreted by priests, not to be 'read' by ordinary people. The Aztecs, as they took power in central Mexico, destroyed many in rewriting history to put themselves in a dominant position, and after them the Spanish destroyed almost all the codices as being full of pagan superstition. Very few have survived. See Appendix by H. von Winning for those held in British institutions.	**Codex (pl. Codices)**
A hard odoriferous resin obtained from various trees, burnt as an offering.	**Copal**
People of Spanish blood born in Mexico. Although they held a high position in Mexican society, from the conquest on, they were excluded from high office in the colonial administration.	***Creoles***

Fresco True fresco is the application of paint onto freshly-applied plaster when the colour is absorbed into the wet plaster.

Frieze Architecturally, the part of the entablature between the architrave and cornice : thus at Acancéh, the stucco frieze filled the façade from above the doorways to the flat roofline.

Frijol Beans, usually kidney beans, a staple food in Mexico, served boiled, mashed and refried as an accompaniment to many dishes.

Garrapatas Ticks, small blood-sucking insects.

Gloss A word or interpretation inserted in the text or margin of a literary work (hence 'glossary').

Glyphs/hieroglyphs Pictoral signs used as script.

Hacienda An estate or plantation, with house and farm buildings.

Ixtaccihuatl 'The White Lady', volcano.

Katunes The title, Katunes of Aké, given by AB to a painting of The Colonnaded Building at Aké: a *katun* is a calendrical cycle of 7,200 days and the beginning or end of a *katun* might be marked by the erection of a commemorative stone. AB perhaps associated the columns of the building with commemorative stones, but there is no evidence for this.

Kekchi A Mayan language still spoken within a small area of Guatemala.

Libation Pouring out of a liquid in honour of, or as an offering to, a god.

Maguey map A large (2410mm x 163mm) map of a suburb of Mexico City, made in the fifteenth or early sixteenth century. Drawn on paper made from maguey or aloe fibre.

Maya long count A means of recording long periods of time in the elaborate calendar of the Maya. The calendar was composed of cycles, all of which interlink like a system of cogwheels. The first short cycle consists of 260 days, the next cycle of 365 days, which together gave a 52-year cycle. This 'Calendar Round' was commonly used for recording dates within the 52-year cycle. Longer periods were recorded by using the Long Count system, which could cover a span of thousands of years calculated from a (?arbitrary) base date. Long count dates are written as a series of units :

144,000 days	=	1 baktun	=	20 katun
7,200 days	=	1 katun	=	20 tun
360 days	=	1 tun	=	18 uinal
20 days	=	1 uinal	=	20 kin
1 day	=	1 kin.		

Thus 9.15.10.0.0. = 30 June AD 741, or 1,407,600 days after the start of the long count on 13 August 3113 BC (Houston, 1989).

Meso-America Central American culture area, which in pre-Conquest times covered the modern countries of Mexico, Guatemala, Belize and parts of Honduras and El Salvador.

Mestizos People of mixed Indian and Spanish blood.

Michoacan 'The place of the masters of fish'.

Mitla 'Place of the Dead'.

Mixcoatl Father of one of the manifestations of Quetzalcoatl.

Mixtec A language spoken in parts of Oaxaca and neighbouring areas in past and present times; also used as a cultural term for the artefacts and archaeological remains produced by Mixtec-speaking peoples.

The language of the Aztecs, used throughout the Aztec empire and still spoken within central Mexico. Many *Nahuatl* words are used in Mexican Spanish. Words like chocolate and tomato came to the English language from *Nahuatl.*	***Nahuatl***
Northern area of the Maya realm, which included the Mexican states of Yucatán, Quintana Roo and part of Campeche. Like the southern Maya, the area was influenced from Mexico.	**Northern Maya**
Volcanic mineral which looks like bottle-glass and was used for tool-making.	**Obsidian**
The people of the first of the great pre-Hispanic cultures.	**Olmec**
In a manuscript, this is where the old writing has been erased and replaced with new writing.	**Palimpsest**
Carved stone club-shaped object, associated with the ritual ball game; *palmas* were carried in a protective yoke-shaped belt worn by players - stone examples of the yokes and *palmas* are common, perhaps replicas of the lighter ones worn by players. The purpose of these pieces is not known; it has been suggested that the stone yokes and *palmas* were worn during play as 'handicaps', or may have been used in ceremonies held before, during or after a game (de Borhegyi 1980).	***Palmas***
Ornament worn on the breast.	**Pectoral**
Bananas.	***Platanos***
A Mayan language still spoken within a small area of Guatemala.	***Pokonchi (Pokomchi)***
'Smoking Mountain', volcano.	**Popocatepetl**
Historical period before the 'discovery' of the Americas by Christopher Columbus in 1492. The Spanish first landed in Mexico in 1519.	**Pre-Columbian**
Fermented drink made from the Maguey plant, a type of aloe (*Agave americana*).	***Pulque***
A range of hills in the Yucatán area; also used for an architectural style which developed in that area during the Late Classic period.	**Puuc**
The feathered serpent, the most important and powerful of the Mexican gods, who was associated with the wind, the dawn and the star Venus and appeared in different manifestations. He was venerated throughout Meso-America. To the Aztecs, he was a hero-god, who created mankind from his own blood and gave them maize to eat. The Maya knew him as Kukulkan; in myth Quetzalcoatl, god/king of the Toltecs, was banished from his kingdom, travelled east and conquered the Maya centre at Chichén Itzá . Toltec myth said that Quetzalcoatl would return and the Spaniard Cortés arrived at the predicted time of this return, so the Aztec king Motecuhzoma failed to act decisively against the Spanish, as he believed the god had returned to destroy the Mexican peoples as legend prophesied.	**Quetzalcoatl**
In wall paintings, codices and carvings, a scroll which issues from the mouth of a figure showing that the figure is speaking - it does not give the words of the speech, like an empty speech bubble in a cartoon.	**Sound scrolls**
Southern area of the Maya realm, which included the highlands of Guatemala and the Mexican state of Chiapas, and the low coastal plain of El Salvador. This area was strongly influenced by Mexican culture.	**Southern Maya**
See sound scroll	**Speech scroll**
Method of taking impressions of relief carvings using wet paper pressed or squeezed onto the relief and allowed to dry.	**Squeeze**
Free-standing stone monument; these are usually carved with a deity or a human figure and a glyphic inscription, with date.	**Stela (pl. stelae)**

Stucco Plaster coating on walls, either to give a smooth finish or for relief moulding.
Tarascan People from the Michoacan area.
Teotihuacán 'The place where men become gods', the Aztec name for the site.
Tlachtli Aztec name for the ball game played throughout central America. It was a game for two teams, the aim being to score goals by passing a rubber ball through a stone ring, the ball being hit only with hips and elbows, not with the hands. *Tlachtli* became a ritual as well as a game - in some games the captain of the losing team (or possibly the winning one) could be sacrificed to the gods.
Tlaloc Rain god, also known as Chac.
Toltec 'The artificers', a people from central Mexico.
Tortillas Maize-flour pancakes, served with most meals.
Tzeltal (Tzaldal) A Mayan language still spoken within a small area of Mexico.
Volan An abbreviation of *volantin*, a horse-drawn vehicle for one or two passengers.
Uxmal Either 'three times built or inhabited' or 'abundant harvest'.
Zapotec 'People of the clouds', people of the Oaxaca area.

Pronunciation

Mexican names can look formidable on the page, but pronunciation is easier when a few rules are followed:

c is a hard consonant, except before *e* and *i*.

h is always silent.

j is pronounced as a guttural *h*, for example, El Ta-hin.

ll is pronounced as a *y*, for example, tor-tee-ya.

ñ is pronounced as *ny*, for example, Pen-ya-feel.

qu is pronounced as *k*.

rr is rolled very strongly.

tl is pronounced like the Welsh *ll*.

u before a vowel is pronounced as *w*, for example, Gwadha-loope.

v is pronounced as *b*.

x is pronounced as *sh*, except between vowels where it pronounced as *h*, for example, Uxmal = OOSH-mal, Oaxaca = Wha-HACK-a.

z is pronounced as a soft *c* or *s*, for example, chee-CHEN eet-SA.

Most of the ancient Mexican names are in *Nahuatl*, the Aztec language, as transcribed by the Spanish *conquistadores*. In *Nahuatl*, the stress is on the penultimate syllable, but Spanish influence means that many are pronounced with the stress on the last syllable, for example, Te-o-tee-WHA-can or Teo-tee-wha-CAN.

Appendix

Pre-Hispanic and early Post-Conquest pictorial manuscripts in British libraries and Museums

Codex Bodley 2858 (Bodleian Library, Oxford)

Mixtec codex relating historical and particularly genealogical events. Painted in 1521 and unfinished due to the Spanish conquest of Oaxaca. Facsimile edition with commentary by Alfonso Caso, in Spanish and English; Sociedad Mexicana de Antropología, Mexico 1958.

Codex Egerton 2895 (British Museum)

Also known as Codex Waecker-Götter, Codex Sánchez Solís, Códice Zapoteco. Completed shortly before or even after the Conquest, glosses in Mixtec. Facsimile edition with introduction by C. A. Burland, Akademische Druck- und Verlagsanstalt, Graz 1965.

Codex Fejérváry-Mayer (National Museums on Merseyside)

One of the best preserved of all Mexican codices; drawings of the figures and symbols are of the highest quality. Important for several religious statements. Facsimile edition with commentary by C. A. Burland. Akademische Druck- und Verlagsanstalt, Graz 1971.

Codex Laud (Ms Laud Misc 678) (Bodleian Library)

A religious manuscript of the so-called Codex Borgian Group, which is the key to the understanding of Pre-Hispanic religion and calendrics. Facsimile edition with commentary by C A Burland, Akademische Druck- und Verlagsanstalt, Graz 1966.

Codex Mendoza (The Collection of Mendoza) (Bodleian Library)

Historical and ethnographic content including a tribute list; with Spanish glosses. Commissioned by Viceroy Mendoza. Colour photo-facsimile with commentaries and English translation of the Spanish text by James Cooper Clark, 3 Vols, London 1938.

Codex Selden 3135 (A.2) (Bodleian Library)

Palimpsest of dynastic histories of a particular Mixtec place. Facsimile edition with commentaries by Alfonso Caso, Sociedad Mexicana de Antropología, Mexico 1964.

The Selden Roll (Bodleian Library)

Sixteenth century mythical or historical narrative, including some ritual elements from western Oaxaca.

Codex Zouche-Nuttall (British Museum)

Pre-Conquest historical account of Mixtec dynasties. Believed to have been sent, together with Codex Vindobonensis (in Vienna), to Charles V by Cortés. Owned by Lord Zouche from whom it was acquired by the British Museum in 1917. Colour reproduction published by the Peabody Museum of American Archaeology and Ethnology, Harvard University, Cambridge, Mass. in 1902. It was accompanied by a booklet written by Zelia Nuttall, titled Codex Nuttall, Facsimile of an Ancient Mexican Codex belonging to Lord Zouche of Harynworth, England.

A paperbound edition appeared in 1975: "The Codex Nuttall, a Picture Manuscript from Ancient Mexico, edited by Zelia Nuttall, with a New Introductory text by Arthur G. Miller, Dover Publications, Inc. New York. [The colour reproduction is inferior to that of the Peabody edition.] The Akademische Druck-und Verlagsanstalt, Graz, published a superb facsimile edition in 1987, "Codex Zouche-Nuttall".

Tepotzotlan Codex (Ulster Museum)

Recently a Mexican Codex on native paper has been found in the Ulster Museum, Belfast. It has been pronounced authentic and is commented on by Gorden Brotherson and Ana Gallegos, "The newly-discovered Tepotzotlan Codex: a first account" In: Recent Studies on Pre-Columbian Archaeology, ed. Nicholas J. Saunders and Olivier de Montmollin, BAR International Series 421(i), 1988,, pp. 205-225.

Bibliography

Andrews, E. Wyllys, IV 1965
Archaeology and Prehistory in the Northern Maya Lowlands: an Introduction
in R. Wauchope and G.R. Willey, 1965, vol. 2, part 1, 288-330
Austin: University of Texas Press

Bell, B. 1971
Archaeology of Nayarit, Jalisco and Colima
in R. Wauchope and G.R. Willey, 1965, vol. 11, 694-753
Austin: University of Texas Press

de Borhegyi, S. 1980
The Precolumbian ballgames: a pan Mesoamerican tradition
Contributions in Anthropology and History No.1
Milwaukee: Milwaukee Public Museum

Brainerd, G.W. 1958
The Archaeological Ceramics of Yucatán
Anthropological Records, no. 19
Berkerley and Los Angeles: University of California

Breton, A.C. 1903
Some Mexican portrait figures
Man, 3, 130-133

Breton, A.C. 1906a
The Wall Paintings at Chichén Itzá
in *Proceedings, 15th International Congress of Americanists,* (Quebec, 1901), 2, 165-169

Breton, A.C. 1906b
Some Notes on Xochicalco
Transactions of the Department of Archaeology (Free Museum of Science and Art), vol. 2(1), 59-68
Philadelphia: University of Pennsylvania

Breton, A.C. 1908
Archaeology in Mexico
Man, 8, 34-37

Breton, A.C. 1910
Extracts from a Report on the Maguey Plan, by Miss Adela Breton
in Diaz del Castillo, B. *The True History of the Conquest of New Spain* vol. III [Trans. Maudslay, A.P.]
London: The Hakluyt Society

Breton, A.C. 1912
Painting and Sculpture in Mexico and Central America
in *Proceedings, 17th International Congress of Americanists* (Buenos Aires, 1910), 1, 245-247

Breton, A.C. 1917
Preliminary Study of the North Building (Chamber C), Great Ball Court, Chich'en itzá, Yucatán
in *Proceedings, 19th International Congress of Americanists,* (Washington DC, 1915), 187-194

Breton, (Lieut.) 1834
Excursions in New South Wales, Western Australia, and Van Dieman's Land during the years 1830, 1831, 1832, and 1833 (2nd ed.)
London: R. Bentley

Bristol Museum and Art Gallery 1924
Annual Report of the Bristol Museum and Art Gallery 1924
Bristol: Bristol Museum

Bristol Museum and Reference Library 1901
Report of the Museum Committee for the year ending 30 September 1900
Bristol: Bristol Museum

British Museum 1923
Guide to the Maudslay Collection of Maya Sculptures (casts and originals) from Central America
London: British Museum

Bullock, W. 1823
Six months residence and travels in Mexico
London: John Murray

Carmichael, E. 1973
The British and the Maya
London: British Museum

Catherwood, F. 1844;1964
Views of ancient monuments in Central America, Chiapas and Yucatán
London: Frances Edwards

Coggins, C. 1984
The Cenote of Sacrifice: Catalogue
in C. Coggins and O.C. Shane III, 1984, 23-166
Austin: University of Texas Press

Coggins, C. and Shane, O.C. III (eds.) 1984
Cenote of Sacrifice: Maya Treasures from the Sacred Well at Chichén Itzá
Austin: University of Texas Press

Chadwick, R. 1971
Archaeological Synthesis of Michoacan and Adjacent Regions
in R. Wauchope and G.R. Willey, 1965, vol. 11, 658-693
Austin: University of Texas Press

Fallaize, E.N. 1923
Obituary. Adela C. Breton
Man, 23 (76), 125

Fernández, M.A. 1939
Exploraciones en Acancéh
in *Actas del 27o Congreso de Americanistas*, vol. II, 249-253
Mexico: Instituto Nacional de Antropología e Historia

Freidel, D.A. n.d.
Children of the First Father's Skull: Terminal Classic Warfare in the Northern Maya Lowlands and the Transformation of Kingship and Elite Hierarchies

[Paper presented at the Symposium 'Mesoamerican Elites: an archaeological assessment', annual meeting of the American Anthropological Association, Chicago, Illinois, November 1987.]

Hammond, N. (ed.) 1977
Social Process in Maya Prehistory: Studies in honour of Sir Eric Thompson
New York: Academic Press

Hirth, K.G. 1982
Transportation Architecture at Xochicalco, Morelos, Mexico
Current Anthropology, 23 (3), 322-4

Holmes, W.H. 1895
Archaeological Studies Amongst the Ancient Cities of Mexico
Field Colombian Museum Anthropological Series, 1(1)
Chicago: Field Colombian Museum

Houston, S.D. 1989
Maya Glyphs
London: British Museum Publications

Kelley, D.H. 1984
The Toltec Empire in Yucatan
The Quarterly Review of Archaeology, March, 12-13

Kingsborough (Viscount) 1831
Antiquities of Mexico comprising fac-similes of ancient Mexican paintings and hieroglyphics
London: Robert Howell & Colnaught Son and Co

Kingsborough (Viscount) 1964
Antiguedades de México, basadas en la recopilación de Lord Kingsborough [reprint]
Mexico: Secretariá de Hacienda y Crédito Público

Kowalski, J. 1985
Lords of the Northern Maya: Dynastic History of Uxmal and Chichen Itza
Expedition, 27 (3), 50-60

Kowalski, J. in press
Who am I among the Itzá? Connections between Northern Yucatán, the Usumacinta - Pasion Drainage, and the Highland Chiapas - Guatemala during the Terminal Classic Period
in R.A. Diehl and J. Berlo (eds.) *Cultural Adjustments in Mesoamerica during and after the Decline of Teotihuacan*
Washington DC: Dumbarton Oaks

Kristan - Graham, C. n.d.
Identification of Lineage in the Art of Chichen Itza
[Paper presented at the Symposium 'Chichén Itzá: Recent advances in Archaeology, Epigraphy and Art History', annual meeting of the Society for American Archaeology, Phoenix, Arizona, April 1988]

Krochock, R. 1988
The Hieroglyphic Inscriptions and Iconography of Temple of the Four Lintels and Related Monuments, Chichén Itzá, Yucatan, Mexico.
Master of Arts thesis
Austin; University of Texas Press

Lincoln, C. 1985
The Chronology of Chichen Itza: a Review of the Literature
in J. Sabloff and E. Wyllys Andrews V (eds.) *Late Lowland Maya Civilisation,* 141-196
Albuquerque: School of American Research

Lincoln, C. n.d.
Dual Kingship at Chichén Itzá
[Paper presented at the Symposium 'Chichén Itzá: Recent advances in Archaeology, Epigraphy and Art History', annual meeting of the Society for American Archaeology, Phoenix, Arizona, April 1988]

Marquina, I. 1951
Arquitectura Prehispánica
Mexico: Instituto Nacional de Antropología e Historia

Maudslay, A.C. and Maudslay A.P. 1899
A Glimpse of Guatemala and Some Notes on the Ancient Monuments of Central America
London: John Murray

Maudslay, A.C. and Maudslay A.P. 1979
A Glimpse of Guatemala and Some Notes on the Ancient Monuments of Central America. [Reprint]
Detroit: Blaine-Ethridge Books

Maudslay, A.P. 1889-1902
Archaeology 5 vols.
in Godman, F.D. and Solvin, O. *Biologia Centrali-Americana*
London: R.H. Porter & Dula

Maudslay, A.P. 1974
Biologia Centrali Americana: Archaeology [facsimile edition]
New York: Milpatron Publishing Corp.

Meighan, C.W. and Nicholson, H.B. 1970
The ceramic mortuary offerings of prehistoric west Mexico: an archaeological perspective
in M. Kan, C. Meighan and H.B. Nicholson *Sculptures of ancient west Mexico; Nayarit, Colima, Jalisco. The Proctor Stafford Collection*
Los Angeles: Los Angeles County Museum of Art

Milbrath, S. n.d.
Astronomical Images and Orientation in the Architecture of Chichén Itzá
[Paper presented at the Symposium 'Chichén Itzá: Recent Advances in Archaeology, Epigraphy and Art History', annual meeting of the Society for American Archaeology, Phoenix, Arizona, April 1988]

Miller, A.G. 1977
Captains of the Itzá: Unpublished Mural Evidence from Chichén Itzá
in N. Hammond 1977, 197-225
New York: Academic Press

Miller, M.E. 1986
The Art of Mesoamerica from Olmec to Aztec
London: Thames and Hudson Ltd

Miller, V. in press
The Frieze of the Palace of the Stuccoes, Acancéh, Yucatán
Washington DC: Dumbarton Oaks

Peñafiel, A. 1890
Monumentos del Arte Mexicano antiquo
Berlin: A Asher and Co

Peñafiel, A. 1900
Teotihuacan: estudio historico y arqueológico
Mexico: Oficina tipográfica de la Secretariá de Fomento

Pendergast, D.M. 1967
Palenque: The Walker-Caddy expedition to the ancient Maya city. 1839-1840
Norman: University of Oklahoma Press

le Plongeon, A. 1896
Queen Moo and The Egyptian Sphinx
London: Kegan Paul & Co

Schele, L. and Miller, M.E. 1986
The Blood of Kings: Dynasty and Ritual in Maya Art
Texas: Kimbell Art Museum, Fort Worth

Seler, E. 1902-1923
Gesammelte Abhandlungen zur Amerikanischen Sprach- und Altertumskunde 5 vols.
Berlin: Ascher, Behrend

Seler, E. 1909
Die Ruinen von Chichén Itzá in Yucatan
in *Proceedings, 16th International Congress of Americanists* (Vienna, 1908)
151-239

Seler, E. 1915a
Die Stuckfacade von Acanceh in Yucatan
in *Seler 1902-1923*, vol.5, 389-404

Seler, E. 1915b
Die Teotihuacan-Kultur des Hochlandes von Mexico
in *E.Seler 1902-1923*, vol.5, 405-585

Stevens, J.L. 1841
Incidents of travel in Central America, Chiapas and Yucatan 2 vols.
New York: Harper and Brothers

Stevens, J.L. 1843
Incidents of travel in Yucatan 2 vols.
New York: Harper and Brothers

Thompson, J.E.S. 1970
Maya History and Religion
Norman: University of Oklahoma Press

Tozzer, A.M. 1930
Maya and Toltec Figures at Chichen Itza
in *Acta 23rd International Congress of Americanists,* (New York, 1928), 155-164

Tozzer, A.M. 1957
Chichen Itza and its Cenote of Sacrifice
in *Memoirs of the Peabody Museum, Harvard University,* vols. 11-12
Cambridge, Massachusetts: Peabody Museum

Wauchope, R. and Willey, G. (eds.) 1965
Handbook of Middle American Indians. Archaeology of Southern Mesoamerica
Austin: University of Texas Press

von Winning, H. 1985
Two Maya monuments in Yucatan: The Palace of the Stuccoes at Acanceh and the Temple of the Owls at Chichén Itzá Anniversary Publication Fund vol. XII
Los Angeles: Southwest Museum

Manuscript Sources

In telling the story of Adela Breton's life and works we are extremely fortunate in two aspects: that Miss Breton was such a prodigious letter writer and, secondly, that several of her letters, and other letters concerning her, have been preserved in various institutions.

The following sources have been used in this publication:

City of Bristol Museum and Art Gallery - BCM
Archival records and letters contained in Historical Files (letter code HF) include letters from AB to the Director(s) and staff of the City Museum on the future of her collections of antiquities; after her death the files contain correspondence to the Museum authorities (including from Professor Tozzer) concerning the rest of her collections of watercolours, photographs, sketchbooks and tracings.

Harvard University Archives - HUA
Miss Breton's letters to F.W.Putnam (Director of the Peabody Museum) and Miss Mead (assistant to Putnam) are in the archive UAV 677z40. Also quoted from this archive are letters from Thompson to Putnam and Bowditch to Putnam.

Peabody Museum of Archaeology and Ethnology - PM
A lengthy correspondence from Miss Breton to Professor Tozzer covering at least 20 years (Tozzer file 5A) and letters from Miss Breton to Bowditch (Bowditch file 41-7) have been utilised in this publication.

Quotations from Miss Breton's letters to the Harvard staff are reproduced by permission of the Harvard University Archives and the Peabody Museum of Archaeology and Ethnology, Harvard University.

List of correspondents

Barker
Alderman W.R. Barker, Chairman of Bristol's Museum Committee from its foundation in 1893 to his death in 1911

Bolton
Dr Herbert Bolton, appointed as Curator of the Bristol Museum in 1898 and retired as Director of the Bristol Museum and Art Gallery in 1930

Bowditch
Charles P. Bowditch, of the Peabody Museum of Archaeology and Ethnology

Mead
Miss Frances Mead, assistant to F.W. Putnam of the Peabody Museum of Archaeology and Ethnology

Putnam
Frederic Ward Putnam, appointed as Curator of the Peabody Museum of American Archaeology and Ethnology in 1875 and retired as Honorary director in 1915

Quick
Richard Quick, Superintendent of the new Bristol Art Gallery and Museum of Antiquities, 1904-1921

Stanton
G.R. Stanton, appointed initially as Assistant Curator and then Curator in Antiquities and Anthropology at Bristol Museum from 1925 to 1951.

Tozzer
Alfred Marston Tozzer, appointed as Instructor in central American Archaeology at Harvard University in 1905 and Curator of Middle American Archaeology at the Peabody Museum in 1914, retiring as Librarian of the Peabody Museum in 1935

Index